This book is dedicated to the men and women of the New Jersey Army and Air National Guard, and their families, who so proudly served during the Persian Gulf War, and in loving memory of our comrade, PFC Tyrone Bowers, 13 Sept. 91.

-The Desert Shield/Storm Family Foundation, Inc.

Symbol of a different culture

Right; Grass that was planted outside of John Shephard's platoon's tent by Joe Vandervort.

Far Right; Thank You! written on wall of American Embassy in Kuwait.

We always remembered what we were there for.

Saudi Emblem.

reminder of how far away home really was, and how important water was in the desert.

Major John Guarascio ("in country")

From all the troops, their families and friends.

Thanks for all your tireless support and effort to us all.

Love

Almost, but not quite. Safe for another while.

Governor Florio and Declan Callan, designer of New Jersey State Desert Storm Medal.

Burning Seas

SPC Mike Spallina getting haircut from
SSG Stagg at TAA near Rafta.

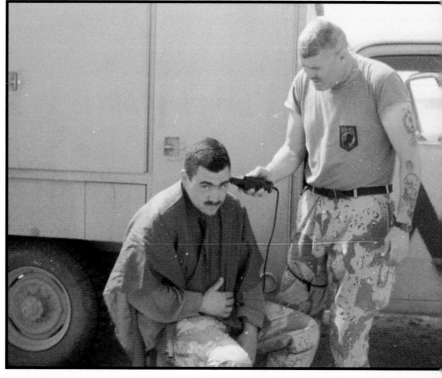

Taking time out on the shore of the Red
Sea.

Top Right; 253rd Lights
out?

Right; SSG Grant
Cunningham and SGT
Joe Klaudi looking for
directions.

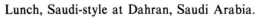

SPC Bryan Wuerker at Kobar Towers on board Iraq's top of the line personnel carrier.

Lunch, Saudi-style at Dahran, Saudi Arabia.

Above left; Christmas necessities arrive in Saudi.

SGT Rondon and the PX manager at the PX in Saudi during Christmas.

BCO on move with MLRS fixing support.

One of hundreds of flaming oil wells.

213th ready to lend aid and support.

Truck #118 moving out from TAA to Razor.

From footprints in the snow to footprints in the sand.

SFC Vey in front of well fire along 6th ring freeway. Taken at 1400 hours on a sunny day

"Water, water everywhere, but not a drop to drink." SPC Joe Vandervort and unknown friend.

"Someone said if we dig for 4 hours, we'll reach Atlantic City." SPC Carlos Scull in the Saudi desert 10 miles from Iraq.

Listening to the radio on the first day of the war.

Bernice Rodriguez at a Saudi oasis.

The War is over! Photo taken after traveling 170 miles in **4** days. SFC McCarty, SFC Panny, SGT Unangst, SGT Godleski, SGT Scott, SFC Dickinson, SPC Ridgway, SPC Stapleton, SPC Blood.

Left; 57mm Iraqi AA gun, overlooking Chike Point.

Below; A brief time for relaxation and rest.

144th system for changing tires!

Hammonton Lions Club members
unveil monument to the 144th.

253rd Christmas Parade float.

144th Easter celebration.

Tears of joy on Homecoming.

253rd Welcome Home celebration.

Desert Storm Rally in Middle Township.

Loading up the heavy equipment.

A farewell from the students of Manchester High School

General Fruscione, Karen Errickson, General Morgano and
Marge Panny at the Merv Griffin's Resorts.

Morning routine Saudi-style.

Everything had to be built from scratch.

National Desert Storm Reservists Day, 1991

By the President of the United States of America

A Proclamation

On this occasion we gratefully salute the members of the National Guard and Reserve forces of the United States—dedicated and highly trained men and women who played a major role in the success of Operation Desert Shield/Desert Storm. Whether they served directly in the Persian Gulf or on military bases in the United States and elsewhere around the world, as members of our Nation's Total Force, these National Guardsmen and reservists made a vital contribution toward the liberation of Kuwait.

During the course of the war in the Persian Gulf, more than 228,000 members of the Ready Reserve were ordered to active duty. Thousands more volunteered in advance of being called to support the coalition effort. Members of the Army National Guard, the Army Reserve, the Naval Reserve, the Marine Corps Reserve, the Air National Guard, the Air Force Reserve, and the Coast Guard Reserve—these men and women were trained and ready to do their jobs. As they have done for all conflicts since colonial times, guardsmen and reservists responded quickly to the call. They promptly assumed a variety of combat missions such as armor, artillery, tactical fighter, tactical reconnaissance, and minesweeping. Their support missions included transportation, medical, airlift, service/supply, civil affairs, intelligence, military police, and communications.

When called to active duty, members of the Ready Reserve were suddenly required to leave behind their families and their careers. As we thank our Desert Storm reservists for the many sacrifices that they have made in behalf of our country, it is fitting that we also honor their loved ones. They too have shown the extraordinary degree of patriotism and courage that we have come to expect of the Nation's military families. National Guard and Reserve units worked in close cooperation with the Active Services to develop a broad-based family support network to assist these new military dependents.

The Nation's employers, educators, and other institutions throughout the private sector have provided strong support and assistance to their reservist employees and students who were called to duty on short notice. The National Committee for Employer Support of the Guard and Reserve, a 4,000-member network of business and civic leader volunteers, has put forth special efforts to help guardsmen and reservists, as well as their employers, to understand their job rights and responsibilities.

In recognition of their vital role in the liberation of Kuwait, the Congress, by Senate Joint Resolution 134, has designated May 22, 1991, as "National Desert Storm Reservists Day" and has authorized and requested the President to issue a proclamation in observance of this day.

NOW, THEREFORE, I, GEORGE BUSH, President of the United States of America, do hereby proclaim May 22, 1991, as National Desert Storm Reservists Day. I call upon all Americans to observe this day with appropriate ceremonies and activities in honor of the courageous men and women of the United States Ready Reserve.

IN WITNESS WHEREOF, I have hereunto set my hand this twenty-first day of May, in the year of our Lord nineteen hundred and ninety-one, and of the Independence of the United States of America the two hundred and fifteenth.

George Bush

JIM FLORIO
GOVERNOR

STATE OF NEW JERSEY
OFFICE OF THE GOVERNOR
CN-001
TRENTON
08625

01 August 1991

To the members of the New Jersey Army and Air National Guard:

On behalf of all the people of New Jersey, I am pleased to extend to all of you, our heartfelt appreciation for your patriotism and dedication.

Your distinguished participation in the Persian Gulf deployment was in the proud tradition of the citizen-soldier. It's a tradition the Guard has lived up to through our state's history.

I thank each of you for your selfless commitment to the defense of our nation and the generous giving of your time and effort in service to your country.

I'm sure you join me in also thanking the family members and colleagues who supported you and waited anxiously for your return.

Lucinda joins me in wishing all of you a very sincere and heartfelt "Welcome Home!" God bless you.

Very Truly Yours,

JIM FLORIO
Governor

Governor Jim Florio/17

How The Crisis Started

Thursday, August 2
At 2 a.m. over 100,000 Iraqi troops invaded the sheikdom of Kuwait.

President Bush immediately described the invasion as "naked aggression."

He then started to enlist the help of world leaders in a collective action against Iraq.

He also banned almost all imports from Iraq and froze Iraqi assets worth over $30 billion in the United States.

President Bush appeared with Mrs. Margaret Thatcher, Prime Minister of Great Britain, in a joint news conference to urge consideration of joint United Nations economic or even military action.

In response, Iraq suspended debt payments to the United States.

Within one hour of the invasion, the United States stepped up air patrols in the Gulf Region and began moving warships, equipment, and supplies from the U.S. military base in Diego Garcia in the Indian Ocean.

Friday, August 3
Iraq said it had set up a "provisional free government" in Kuwait and would start to withdraw its troops on Sunday, as long as no one interfered.

Iraqi troops moved closer to the border of Saudi Arabia.

Sunday, August 5
Secretary of Defense Dick Cheney travelled to Saudi Arabia to meet with Saudi leaders to discuss options for handling the crisis.

Monday, August 6
The United Nations Security Council voted 13-0 to impose a sweeping ban on trade with Iraq.

President Bush and Prime Minister Thatcher praised the UN action and spoke of the possibility of a naval blockade if economic sanctions are not effective.

Tuesday, August 7
President Bush ordered U.S. military troops and aircraft to Saudi Arabia after King Fahd approved the deployment of a multinational force to defend Saudi Arabia against Iraqi forces in Kuwait.

Iraqi President Saddam Hussein angrily rejected foreign pressure for Iraqi forces to pull out of Kuwait. He bitterly attacked the rule of royal families and defended the invasion of Kuwait as necessary to correct the flawed regional borders drawn by colonial powers.

Operation DESERT SHIELD

August 8
The Division Ready Brigade of the 82d Airborne Division left Fort Bragg, North Carolina, at 3:00 a.m. EDT for Saudi Arabia to take up defensive positions as directed by President George Bush.

August 9
Pentagon officials announced that elements from the 24th Infantry Division (Mechanized), Fort Stewart, Georgia, and elements of the 101st Airborne Division (Air Assault), Fort Campbell, Kentucky, which includes aviation assets, will be sent to the Persian Gulf region.

August 10
Elements of the 24th Infantry Division (Mechanized) began movement by road and rail to the port of Savannah to load vehicles and equipment aboard U.S. Navy Fast Scalift Ships (FSSs).

August 11
Elements of the 101st Airborne Division (Air Assault) began movement to Jacksonville, Florida, for embarkation for deployment to the Middle East.

August 12
Elements of the 11th Air Defense Artillery Brigade, Fort Bliss, Texas, equipped with the "Patriot" and "Stinger" anti-aircraft missiles, deployed to Southwest Asia.

August 13
The Fast Scalift Ship USNS Capella sailed at 12:57 pm EDT from Savannah, bound for the Middle East, carrying vehicles and equipment of the 24th Infantry Division (Mechanized).

August 14
A large contingent of FORSCOM Reserve volunteers begin arriving at installations and ports of debarkation in the United States to augment combat service and combat service support units.

August 15
Units of 1st Corps Support Command, stationed at Fort Bragg, and the 197th Infantry Brigade (Mechanized), Fort Benning, Georgia, began deploying to the Middle East.

August 16
Elements of the 3d Armored Calvary Regiment, Fort Bliss, Texas, began deployment to the Middle East.

August 17
Elements of the 1st Calvary Division and 2d Armored Division, both based at Fort Hood, Texas, began preparation for deployment to the Middle East as part of Operation DESERT SHIELD.

August 18
Elements of the 101st Aviation Brigade, Fort Campbell, Kentucky, began arriving in the Middle East.

August 22
President Bush, acting under the authority of Title 10, Section 673 B of the United States Code, authorized the Secretary of Defense to call members of the Selected Reserve to active duty status. These Reservists will support Operation Desert Shield by joining active duty units deployed in and around the Arabian peninsula or by filling critical military support vacancies in the United States or elsewhere.

August 23
The Army announced that elements of III Corps Artillery, Fort Sill, Oklahoma, are deploying to the Middle East.

August 24
Selected units of the Army National Guard and Army Reserve were alerted for possible call-up to active duty in support of Operation DESERT SHIELD.

August 25
The Pentagon announced 174 FORSCOM Reserve Component units will be activated from 38 states and Puerto Rico. Those FORSCOM units include Army Reserve and, when federalized, Army National Guard.

August 26
The 1st Calvary Division; 2d Brigade, 2d Armored Division; and 3d Armored Calvary Regiment continue to load for employment to Saudi Arabia.

August 27
At 3:00 p.m. local time, equipment of the 24th Infantry Division began to unload from the USNS Capella in Saudi Arabia.

MG Vito Morgano
Adjutant General

State of New Jersey

DEPARTMENT OF MILITARY AND VETERANS' AFFAIRS

EGGERT CROSSING ROAD, CN 340
TRENTON, NEW JERSEY 08625-0340

JIM FLORIO
GOVERNOR
COMMANDER-IN-CHIEF

1 August 1991

VITO MORGANO
MAJOR GENERAL
THE ADJUTANT GENERAL

To the Members of the New Jersey National Guard:

As The Adjutant General and Commander of both the Army and Air National Guard, I am extremely proud of the professionalism and esprit de corps demonstrated by the outstanding men and women of our units who participated in Desert Shield/Desert Storm.

Your exceptional performance put to rest once and for all any questions as to the military readiness, professional ability or personal commitment to our national defense of units or individuals within the Reserve Component.

Each of you was presented with a challenge--each of you responded admirably. I commend your patriotism, pride and the self-sacrifice you endured in answering our nation's call to arms.

No Commander could be more pleased or more proud of your performance, conduct or courage. You have, indeed, acquitted yourselves in a manner befitting the honorable traditions of both the New Jersey National Guard and the Armed Forces of the United States.

VITO MORGANO
Major General, NJARNG
The Adjutant General

Brig. Gen. Preston Taylor
Deputy Adjutant General

Richard Bernard
Deputy Commissioner
Veteran's Affairs

Talking Points:

Operation Desert Shield

The U.S. Army

- The Army is a Total Force—the Active Component and the Reserve Component (Army National Guard and Army Reserves).

- 50 percent of the Army's combat capability is in the Reserve Component.

- 70 percent of the Army's combat service support capability is in the Reserve Component.

- Operations in the Persian Gulf will be austere, with long supply and transportation lines.

- The Army must be ready to sustain long-term operations.

- The Army is a strategic force, and must maintain its presence in Europe and the Pacific. It must also maintain a contingency force in CONUS.

United States Central Command

- U.S. forces are one part of a multi-national force assembled in defense of threats to worldwide vital interests.

- U.S. forces are present in Saudi Arabia to set up defensive positions and then to train and work with the Saudi military units and others as appropriate.

- America does not seek conflict, nor does it seek to chart the destiny of other nations, but America will stand by her friends. The mission of U.S. troops is wholly defensive.

- U.S. troops are not in Saudi Arabia to drive the Iraqis out of Kuwait; the economic sanctions are designed to accomplish that goal.

- This is a joint U.S. and multi-national effort as personnel from all the U.S. services, Saudi Arabia, and other countries are assembled.

Directorate of Public Affairs
Headquarters, Forces Command
Fort McPherson, Ga. 30330-6000

Bulletin 1-90
23 Aug 90

Air National Guard

Operation Desert Shield/Storm Facts

- More than 800 personnel were mobilized from 10 Air Guard aeromedical evacuation units.

- Aeromedical activity in SWA supported 979 litter patients and 1,559 ambulatory patients.

- A typical example from the initial days of the operation involved a request to the 167th Tactical Airlift Group, a C-130 unit from Martinsburg, West Virginia. A late evening call to the unit for forty aerial port personnel to voluntarily deploy in support of air cargo operations was answered in a few hours with over 100 volunteers.

- By the time the Presidential 200,000 personnel call-up was initiated, more than 2,700 Air National Guard men and women were voluntarily serving in critical mission areas in support of Desert Shield.

- The first U.S. aircraft flown into Southwest Asia was an Air National Guard (ANG) C-141 from the 172d Military Airlift Group of Jackson, Mississippi.

- In the first month, the total airlift was almost twice the amount lifted during the peak month of the Vietnam war and three times as much and more than triple the distance as Operation Just Cause in Panama.

- Before any ANG unit was activated, ANG volunteers flew strategic airlift C-5s and C-141s into the theater. Additionally, 16 C-130 tactical airlift aircraft, 16 KC-135 refueling aircraft, 6 RF-4 reconnaisance aircraft, and 2 EC-130 special operations aircraft were flown and maintained by ANG volunteers in the theater of operations.

- 12,270 Air Guardsmen and women served in Operation Desert Storm.
    - 1,145 were volunteers
    - 5,118 served in Southwest Asia
    - 5,315 performed duties in the USA
    - 692 served in other overseas areas

New Jersey Army National Guard
General Officers

BG Richard Schneider
50th Armor Division General

BG Robert J. Byrne
Assistant Division Commander

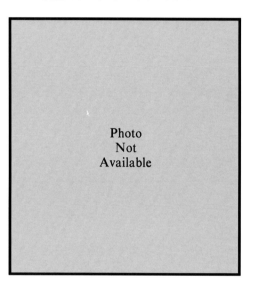

Photo
Not
Available

BG William S. Greenberg
Asst. Adjutant General - Army

BG Santo Fruscione
Deputy STARC Commander

CSM Richard T. LaRocca
State Command Sergeant Major

Col. Dominick Trocchia
Commander, Troop Command

New Jersey Air National Guard
General Officers

Maj. Gen. Edward Philbin
Commander, NJ Air National Guard

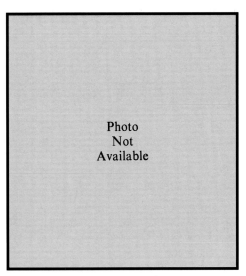

Brig. Gen. Neil D. Kennedy
Deputy Commander, NJ Air National Guard

Brig. Gen. Robert V. Paschon
Asst. Adjutant General - Air

Colonel (P) R. Craig Cosgrave
Cdr. 108th Tactical Fighter Wing

Colonel James McIntosh
Cdr. 170th Air Refueling Group

Colonel Tom Griffin
Cdr. 177 Fighter Interceptor Group

Operation Desert Shield:

"A Line In The Sand"

Principles Guiding U.S. Policy:

"First, we seek the immediate, unconditional and complete withdrawal of all Iraqi forces from Kuwait.

Second, Kuwait's legitimate government must be restored to replace the puppet regime.

Third, my administration, as has been the case with every administration from President Roosevelt to President Reagan, is committed to the security and stability of the Persian Gulf.

Fourth, I am determined to protect the lives of American citizens abroad."

—President George Bush

Purpose Statement:

"Specifically, our purpose in sending forces at this time to the Gulf region, and to Saudi Arabia in particular, is to deter any further Iraqi aggression; also to work with Saudi forces to improve their military and defensive capabilities; and should it become necessary, should deterrence fail, to defend Saudi Arabia against attack."

—Secretary of Defense Dick Cheney

Mission Statement:

"U.S. forces will work together with those of Saudi Arabia and other nations, to preserve the integrity of Saudi Arabia, and to deter further aggression. Through their presence as well as through training and exercises, these multinational forces will enhance the overall capability of Saudi armed forces to defend the kingdom."

—General H. Norman Schwarzkopf
Commander-in-Chief
United States Central Command

Directorate of Public Affairs
Headquarters, Forces Command
Fort McPherson, Ga. 30330-6000

Bulletin 2-90
27 Aug 90

STATE OF NEW JERSEY
DEPARTMENT OF MILITARY AND VETERANS' AFFAIRS
EGGERT CROSSING ROAD, CN 340
TRENTON, NEW JERSEY 08625-0340

ARMY BULLETIN NO. 51   25 March 1991
AIR BULLETIN NO. 26

(Effective until 25 March 1993
unless sooner rescinded or superseded)

DESERT STORM   (CAO/ESO)

Reference TWX msg 131030Z Mar 91, SAB, from General Conaway is quoted as follows:

1. "It is times such as these when words hardly seem adequate to convey the appreciation and admiration of a grateful nation. My heartfelt thanks and congratulations to the more than 75,000 members of the Army and Air National Guard federalized in support of Operations Desert Shield and Desert Storm. In the spirit of the original minuteman, guardmembers from all walks of life left families and civilian jobs to answer the call of the nation.

2. The professionalism and dedication that has been the hallmark of your service in the National Guard contributed immensely to the great military success of Desert Storm. In support and combat roles, Guard units performed vital missions.

3. To our fallen comrades in arms, we offer our prayers. To their loved ones, we offer our support and sympathy and the assurance that they will remain in our hearts and memories. To the families, it is important for them to know that the sacrifice of their loved ones was not in vain. And to those who have returned, it is forever important that we honor those who paid the ultimate price of victory.

4. Each and every Guard family placed a critical role in Desert Shield and Storm. From providing support to deployed family members while waiting anxiously on the home front, to the countless hours helping and supporting the thousands of families in need of assistance during those trying times--the family, as always, provided the bedrock foundation for the spirit and winning attitude of the warriors.

5. To the soldiers and airmen, know that you are forever changed, touched by what you have seen, shaped by what you have experienced, bonded with those whom with you have shared this trial. Know in your heart, most importantly, you were and forever will be equal to the challenge--you are Americans at their best.

6. God bless you, the National Guard and the Great Nation we all serve proudly."

OFFICIAL: VITO MORGANO
                                               Major General, NJARNG
                                               The Adjutant General

NICHOLAS C. KING
Major, NJANG (Ret)
Chief, Administrative Services

DISTRIBUTION:
A,A2,A3,B,C,D,E

THE VICE PRESIDENT
WASHINGTON

July 22, 1991

Dear Friends:

It is an honor and a pleasure to extend my warmest thanks for a job well done in Operation Desert Storm.

This is a time of great pride for America. A new sense of optimism and patriotism has been reborn in America, and I know I speak for millions of Americans when I express this nation's appreciation for your courageous service in the liberation of Kuwait. For your contributions to the survival of liberty in the world, each of you merits a special thanks from all the freedom-loving people of the world.

Throughout our nation's history, Americans have always answered the call to protect and defend the friends of liberty in the face of aggression. America truly stands united behind her troops, and all Americans give thanks not only to you, our Desert Storm veterans, but also to all American veterans who have served this great nation over the years.

We must also remember that there have always been those Americans who have made the ultimate sacrifice in opposing aggression. In their memory, we must never forget that the price of peace is always high and that the defense of liberty is an unceasing task.

With that in mind, let us give thanks for the many blessings and liberties that we as Americans enjoy. The magnificent allied victory in the Persian Gulf conflict gives us the opportunity to rededicate ourselves to the principles upon which this nation was founded -- freedom, democracy, and the rule of law.

Marilyn and I will continue to keep you and your families in our thoughts and in our prayers. May God bless you for all that you have done for the cause of peace, and may He continue to bless this great nation of ours.

Sincerely,

Dan Quayle

2 August 1991

To the Desert Shield/Desert Storm Family Foundation,

I'm honored to have this opportunity to commend all the outstanding soldiers, airmen, and families of New Jersey's Army and Air National Guard who served in Operations Desert Shield and Desert Storm. Congratulations on a job well done!

As members of America's National Guard, you are part of a distinguished tradition that dates back to the colonial militia. In virtually every major conflict, civil disturbance, or natural catastrophe since the Revolutionary War, our Guard has stood ready and answered when duty called. I'm very proud to report that the results of Operation Desert Storm proved that the pride, professionalism, dedicated service, and commitment to the ideals of our nation that have always been the hallmark of our National Guard once again burned brightly.

As the Desert Shield/Desert Storm Family Foundation of New Jersey commemorates these brave Army and Air National Guard heroes, let us all look back in gratitude at the achievements of our veterans and forward with hope for a lasting world peace. God bless you.

Sincerely,

H. NORMAN SCHWARZKOPF
General, U.S. Army

General Schwarzkopf

August 1991

**To the Men and Women of New Jersey Who
Served in Operations Desert Shield/Desert Storm**

As you look through the pages of this yearbook, I know the pride and sense of accomplishment you feel will be enhanced by the sure knowledge that the people of New Jersey created such a fine tribute to you. It was such magnificent support, from all across America, that enabled us to achieve such a spectacular victory in the Gulf.

But it was also the dedication, courage, and devotion to duty which you displayed that gave us that victory. Without your skills, your bravery, your sense of purpose and mission, there could have been no liberation of Kuwait. So take pride in what you accomplished. The momentous events you see happening around the world today -- unprecedented U.S.-Soviet cooperation, new democracies forming at all points of the globe, historic arms control agreements, and much, much more -- would not have been possible without the dedicated service of all of you and of the over two million other men and women in our Armed Forces who are just like you.

This yearbook is for you. Look through it with the full knowledge that you have helped make a new order take shape in the world. And I am very proud of all of you.

Sincerely,

COLIN L. POWELL
Chairman
Joint Chiefs of Staff

EXECUTIVE ORDER NO. 15

WHEREAS, the President of the United States issued an Executive Order on August 22, 1990, authorizing the Secretary of Defense to call up select members of the Reserve and National Guard to active duty during the Middle East crisis and authorizing the Secretary of Transportation to similarly call up members of the Coast Guard Reserve;

WHEREAS, Reserve and National Guard members who are activated during this crisis serve a vital national interest for which they deserve the full support of the citizens of this State;

WHEREAS, the State of New Jersey recognizes that a strong, ready Reserve and National Guard are essential to the defense of this country and vital to this State in time of emergency or natural disaster;

WHEREAS, the State of New Jersey encourages its employees to serve in the Reserve and National Guard and recognizes the personal and economic sacrifices of its employees who are called to active duty during the Middle East crisis;

NOW, THEREFORE, I, JAMES J. FLORIO, Governor of the State of New Jersey, by virtue of the authority vested in me by the Constitution and by the Statutes of this State, do hereby Order and Direct:

1. New Jersey State employees who are called to active duty during the Middle East crisis shall be entitled upon termination of active duty to return to State employment with full seniority and benefits consistent with State and federal military reemployment and seniority rights.

2. During active duty for a total of up to 180 days, these State employees shall be entitled to receive a salary equal to the differential between the employee's State salary and the employee's military pay.

3. These State employees shall be entitled to State employee health benefits, life insurance and pension coverage during active duty service for which they receive differential salary as prescribed in this order as if they were on paid leave of absence.

4. The Commissioner of Personnel shall implement this Executive Order and each department, office, division or agency of the State is authorized and directed, to the extent not inconsistent with law, to cooperate with the Commissioner of Personnel and to make available to him such information, personnel and assistance as necessary to accomplish the purposes of this Order.

5. This Order shall take effect immediately.

GIVEN, under my hand and seal this
17 day of SEPT
in the Year of Our Lord, one thousand nine hundred and ninety, and of the Independence of the United States, the two hundred and fifteenth.

JAMES J. FLORIO
GOVERNOR

Attest:

_____

John A. Sweeney
Counsel to the Governor

170th Air Refueling Group

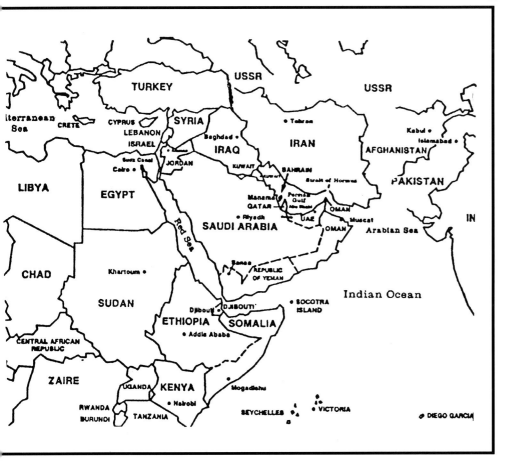

the maintainers from the 170th Consolidated Aircraft Maintenance Squadron received the first calls. The unit mission requirements were changed to reflect additional Strategic Air Command Alert responsibilities throughout the United States and the continued support of the "Air Bridge".

As operations continued, so did the mobilizations. The following units were mobilized:

Unit	# of personnel	Month/Yr	Assignment
170th USAF Clinic	16	Feb 91	Several Conus Bases
170th Services Flight	17	Feb 91	F.E. Warren AFB WY
170th Security Police	44	Feb 91	Minot AFB ND

Throughout Operation Desert Shield/Storm, many individuals, although not mobilized, made continuous and significant contributions to the successes of the 170th's participation in this "Desert Victory". Members from both base Air National Guard Finance and Consolidated Personnel functions were there to meet the flow of outgoing and incoming flights. The support from other staff agencies such as the Staff Judge Advocate, the Chaplain and especially the 170th Mission Support Flight was outstanding and just as vital to the success of the mission. Disaster Preparedness and the Combat Arms personnel increased the frequency and intensity of their training. Thanks to them, all deployed members reinforced their confidence to operate in a hostile chemical environment. Many members served voluntary tours of duty at bases throughout the United States, including several who served directly at major command levels, on tour with the Air National Guard Support Center, Strategic Air Command, and Tactical Air Command.

The participation of the 170th Air Refueling Group came to a happy and successful conclusion with the return and demobilization of the 170th Services Flight from F.E. Warren AFB, Wyoming on 3 July 91. Approximately 300 guardsmen were active in Operations Desert Shield and Desert Storm. This included 141 who were mobilized. Several men and women successfully completed multiple volunteer tours of duty and were mobilized as well.

It was a job well done. Our unit motto is "Global Readiness". Thanks to our training, abilities and response, the 170th Air Refueling Group was and remains "Globally Ready"!

The 170th Air Refueling Group launched one of the first KC-135E Stratotankers of Operation Desert Shield. This occurred on 2 August 1991 at the very dawn of air operations to establish the "Air Bridge" to the Southwest Asia Theater. This mission of extreme importance had to be performed concurrently with others critical to the national defense of the United States of America. Personnel assigned to the 150th Air Refueling Squadron and the 170th Consolidated Aircraft Maintenance Squadron deployed rapidly throughout the world to United States Air Force bases. Tankers from the 170th Air Refueling Group assisted in the mission to refuel hundreds of eastward bound aircraft as the rapid build-up occurred.

The men and women of the 170th Air Refueling Group were active participants in provisional wings from August to December 1990. Aircrews, maintainers and support personnel were assigned to the 1701st Air Refueling Wing (P) in Saudi Arabia in volunteer Temporary Duty tours ranging from two weeks to thirty days. Members of the 170th Consolidated Aircraft Maintenance Squadron and the 170th Security Police Flight volunteered for duty with the 801 Air Refueling Wing (P) at Moron AB in Spain. With the guidance of the Logistics and Planning office, 170th members were integrated into units on these rotational tours with other Air National Guard, Air Force Reserve and Active Duty units.

December, 1990 witnessed the first mobilizations of 170th personnel as plans for Operation Desert Storm were coming close to implementation. The aircrews of the 150th Air Refueling Squadron and

170th Air Refueling Group

170SPF

TSG DARE
TSG LOWERY
MSG LUCAS
MSG CODISPOTI
AIC ADLER
AB ALBINO
SSG BANKS
SGT BEUN D
SGT BEUN M
AJC BLUMBERG
SRA BROSIUS
SSG BRUYNELL
SSG COLIAO
AMN COOPER
SGT DARBY
SGT EDWARDS
AIC FAHNESTOCK
SRA FEDE
SRA FIELDS
TSG FORMAN
SRA GLEASON
SRA FIELDS
SSG GREGG T
AIC HOCEK
SGT JAMIESON
SSG KUO
SSG LEAHY
SSG LOMON

SSG GREGG
SGT MARSHALL H
AIC MARSHALL P
SRA MISSELHORN
SGT MITCHELL
SSG MOORE
TSG MORTON
AIC NAPP
SGT LYONS
SSG PRZYBYLSKI G
SSG PRZYBYLSKI T
SSG SANTIAGO
SGT SCANNELL
SGT TRAD
SRA WILLIAMS
SSG DELGADO

170CL

TSG EDWARDS
SSG HAWKINS
SSG WIMBERLY
1LT WIMBERLY
LTC WETSTEIN
SSG PLEASENT
LTC FREIDMAN
TSG QUINTANA
SRA SANDERS
SSG PENA
TSG SKOWRONSKI

SSG THORNHILL
AIC MOCHEL
SSG CONZO
MAJ CRAIG
TSG SALTER
SMS GORGA

170 GP

LTC CORNS

170 CAMS

* CONUS PERSONNEL

SGT MCDONALD
SSG CRUZ
TSG FRYE *
TSG KELSCH *
SSG DEMPSEY *
TSG SUSEN
MSG PARSONS
TSG HOPKINS
TSG MOERTL
SSG MORTON *
SGT GONZALEZ *
TSG CZAPLINSKI *

SSG NEAL *
MSG KAELIN *
SSG PAULIN *
MSG HORN *
TSG MILLS *
SSG MURPHY *
TSG ROZIER
TSG HUTCHINSON
MSG CIRELLI
AIC GREEN
TSG BARRICELLI
TSG KALINUK
TSG SHIVELY
TSG BERGERON
MSG KAELIN

170SVF

SSG SCHWARTZ
TSG BROWN
SSG BROWN
SRA MODESTINO
TSG BROWN
TSG JONES
SSG HARRIS
SSG PRICE
SGT HOLMAN

C130 on the Tarmac

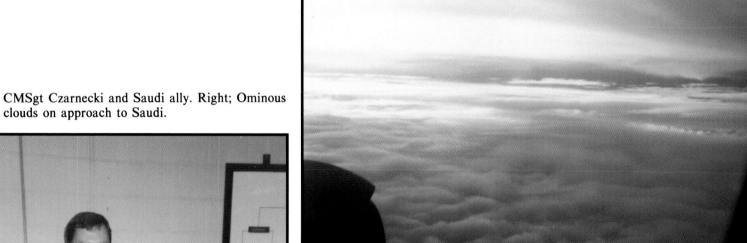

CMSgt Czarnecki and Saudi ally. Right; Ominous clouds on approach to Saudi.

170th in Refueling operations.

CMSgt. Czarnecki and family.

In-Country.

The tension mounts on the flight over.

The 170th In-Processing.

Maj. Scheaffer and TSgt. Cremer.

170th

Colonel and Mrs. James McIntosh.

The 170th Security Police Flight.

170th In-Processing.

Below left; In-Processing and family briefing.

Below; Maj. Dickinson and Maj. Sheaffer.

CMSgt. Czarnicki and
Maj. Halliday look over
holiday greeting card.

Maj. Halliday checks out
the quickest way home.

In-Country quarters.

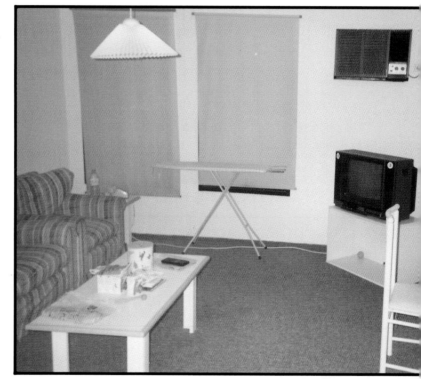

CMSgt. Czarnicki stands in front of "Sand drags" sign.

City street doesn't quite look like home.

Some accomodations were very different.

Sgt. Paul Fede of the 170 Security Police guards Stealth Fighter at Moron AF, Spain.

170 Air Refueling Group loads up.

SSgt Moore and Family at Homecoming.

Vice Commander Colonel Hugh Wilson
and Governor Jim Florio on the Governor's
Press Tour.

The 170 Clinic.

TSgt. Dzierzynski points out symbols for successful refueling missions.

MSgt. Cirelli debarks from plane in full Arab regalia.

SSgt. Delgade gets "Welcome Home."

**(left to right) SPC Jay Cee Dixon, SGT Gary Stoeffler
2LT Michael McLean (Commander), & SFC Frank Marchetti**

328th Transportation Detachment

On September 23, 1990, the 328th Transportation Detachment, a four man unit, was put on alert for mobilization to Saudi Arabia. On September 27, 1990, the mobilization occurred and the unit reported to the Pemberton Armory, its permanent base of operations.

After a three day period at the Pemberton location, the 328th Transportation Detachment reported to Fort Dix, NJ, for further training and Middle East briefings. The unit left Fort Dix on October 9, 1990, and their first stop was Torresjon AFB, Spain, for refueling. They finally arrived in Dahran, Saudi Arabia on October 10th.

For the next three and one half months, until the air war began, the 328th coordinated and monitored all convoys on the Northeastern Saudi Arabian border (MSR's) highways in support of the 18th Airborne Corps.
On February 25, 1991, this unit entered Iraq 2 hours after the ground war started. Our mission again was to coordinate all convoys with essential cargo, ammo, food, water, spare parts were all our top priorities. After almost a month in Iraq, the 328th was sent to Kuwait to continue the monitoring of critical points along the MSR's.

Our higher headquarters was the 330th Movement Control Center out of Fort Bragg, N.C. The 328th Transportation Detachment travelled in excess of 27,000 miles during their 7 month, 16 days of active duty.

The Commander of the 330th MCC praised the 328th during this campaign for their outstanding job and devotion to duty during the Gulf War. In his letter to the Adjutant General of the State of New Jersey, Department of Veterans and Military Affairs, he stated that the 328th Transportation Detachment performed their mission with excellence.

The 328th Transportation Detachment left Saudi Arabia on April 17, 1991, for a first stop at Sicily, Italy, and a second stop at Shannon, Ireland, and then on to the final stop in the U.S.A. in Philadelphia.

Friends

President and Mrs. George Bush
Vice Pres. & Mrs. Dan Quayle
Governor and Mrs. Jim Florio
MG Vito and Louise Morgano
Brig. Gen. & Mrs. Preston Taylor
50th Armor Div. Headquarters
NJ Air Nat. Guard Headquarters
The Clayton Powell Family
The Schwarzkopf Family
NJ Family Program Office
News Tribune, Woodbridge
Donco Graphics, Landisville
PMA Foundation, Philadelphia
Kindle Ford, CM Ct. House
VVA Chapter #228
Quick Check Food Stores
ABBIAMO, Hammonton
Starns Shop Rite
Cape May Cares
Women's Club Of Absecon
Welcome Home 144th J & D Keough
Arnold/Dorothy Caslin
SSG Bob & Pat Calkins & Family
The Goddard Family
The Feldhann Family
Eliz, Peter, Nicole, Rebe Yull
The Goldstein Family
The Falcones - Welcome Home!!!
Ruth Burroughs/SGT. Wm. Gaskill
BG S.J. Fruscione, DSC
The Keisers - Welcome Home 144
SSG & Mrs. Joseph G. Ellis
Dolores and SGT Paul Nichols
Gagliardi Family - We Love You
SFC & Mrs. Michael Vey
SFC Joseph A. Lyons, Jr.
CPT Robert Springer And Family
The Hughes Bud Sue & The Boys
Harry Alex Martin III
Leon & Jo Ann Wescoat
Flight Line Restaurant
Nat'l Jr. Honor Soc. Ocean City
Nabisco Brands, Inc.
Thanks! J.E. Klaudi's Family
Welcome Back Dee-Job Well Done
SGM & Mrs. Michael T. Hughes
Mr/Mrs John Munford Sr/Family
Robin Tom Will Tiff Ed Unc Joe
Party Poopers Of Northfield NJ
154 S & S Officers Assn

1st Steps back in USA

328th preparing to deploy to
Saudi Arabia

Gary during an equipment
check "in country"

Proud to be a New Jersean

The ground war has begun Iraq & Saudi Border

Somewhere in Northern Saudi Arabia

"In Country"

Gary & Jay Cee in Desert

328th

1LT McClean meets son for the 1st time

ank and Mike getting off plane in
iladelphia

52/253rd Transportation Company

253rd Transportation Company

On September 27, 1990 the 253rd Transportation Company from Cape May Court House was activated to duty. On Sunday, September 30th, the unit and their trucks convoyed up the Parkway to Ford Dix for processing and training. The advance team left for Saudi Arabia on November 7th with a stop over in Spain for refueling and maintenance and finally arrived in Dahran, Saudi Arabia on November 22th. The main body left on November 8th with a stop over in Germany and arrived in Saudi Arabia on November 9th.

The unit's first home was at the port of Damaan where they were housed in a large warehouse along the docks. For the next 2 months the 253rd, while assigned to the 68th Transportation Battalion, hauled supplies, ammo and mail forward to the combat units particularly the 1st Calvary Division and the 24th Infantry Division.

On January 17, the 253rd was attached to the 2nd Brigade of the 82nd Airborne. The mission of the 1st Platoon, along with a detached squad from the 3rd platoon was to transport the infantry of the 4th BN, 325th Infantry for ground combat operations into Iraq. The 2nd platoon, along with a detached squad from the 1122 Transportation Company, Arkansas National Guard was assigned the same duties but with the 2nd BN, 325 Infantry. The remainder of the company was assigned to the Battalion Support Area (BSA).

253rd Transportation Company

CPT Daniel O. Errickson, Company Commander

1LT Christopher A. Brown
1LT Edward Sherretta
2LT William L. Peace
WO Wayne Grega

1SG Stephen Barna, Jr., First Sergeant

SSG Waymond Adcock
SGT Vanya Bailey
SPC Edward Barnes
SPC Robert Baxter
SGT Ceasar Bennett
SPC Tracey Berry
SPC Ernest Blood
SSG John Bordley
SPC Edward Bryant
SGT John Burgess
SPC Douglas Cabler
SPC Anthony Caffrey
SSG Robert Calkins
SSG Edward Camp
SPC Miguel Castillo
SGT Dawn Crouse
SPC Patrick Day
SFC Salvator DeGirolamo
SPC Jessee Diaz
PFC Gregory Dick
SPC David Dickinson
SPC Joseph Dicola
SPC Luis Flores
SGT John Ford
SGT Sharon Freed
SPC Donald Fulk
PFC Kikiea Fuller
SGT Emanuel Fulton
SGT William Gaskill
SPC Sean Gautier
SPC Glenn Godleski
SPC Frank Goodwin
PFC Felicia Greene
PFC Julie Guerdgiel
SPC Kevin Harkins
SPC Dwayne Hemphill
SGT Lisa Higgs
SSG Francis Holland
SPC Joseph Horn

SPC Joseph Hunt
SPC Fred Jackson
SGT Theodore Jackson
SPC Peter Jacques
SPC William Jarmon
SPC Richard Johnson
SPC William Jorgenson
SGT Daniel Julio
SGT Marcelino Julio
SPC William Kaelin
SSG Ronald Kent
SSG John Kill
SPC Mark Leonard
SPC Timothy Lewis
SSG Brian L'Italian
SFC Ralph Lonergan
SSG Stanley Longo
SPC Manuel Maldonado
SPC Sean Maloney
SSG Joseph Marchina
SGT Harry Martin
SPC Roger Marvin
SFC William McCarty
SPC James McCourt
SPC Gordon McCourt
SPC Garry McMichael
SPC Frederick Merkel
SPC Milton Mickel
SGT Veronica Miller
SPC Kevin Money
SPC David Moyer
SGT John Mulcahy
SPC Lawrence Murdock
SGT John Newlin
SSG Robert Padilla
SPC Clayton Palmer
SFC Edward Panny
SGT Roseanne Polini
SPC Ronald Poole

SGT Peter Quinlan
SPC Rory Racela
SPC Bradley Rance
SGT Curtis Randall
SPC Scott Ridgeway
SPC Edward Riggin
SGT Morris Riland
SPC Juan Rivera
SPC John Robinson
SGT Cesar Rondon
PFC Ralph Robertshaw
SGT Michael Savage
SGT Francis Scott
SPC Carlos Scull
PFC Alfred Shumate
SSG Francis Sippel
SPC Thomas Sippel
SPC Wayne Solomon
SPC Michael Spallina
SGT Joseph Spinicchia
SPC Steven Splatt
SSG James Stagg
SPC Thomas Stapleton
SSG Edward Szotak
SGT Joseph Tedesco
SGT Charles Unangst
SSG Andrew Vaden
SFC Michael Vey
SPC Charles Vogel
SSG Kelvin Walker
SPC James Weed
PFC William Webber
SPC Vincent White
SPC David Williams
SPC Frank Wolbert
PFC Karl Woodeshick
SPC Bryan Wuerker
SGT George Yakstis

e May Pull-Out Farewell

James McCourt packing to go

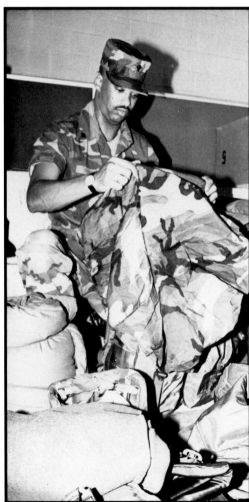

SP4 Bryant packing

Middle photo) SP4 Horn (left) & Sgt. Lorretta (right) during In-Processing
Bottom photo) SFC Lonergan giving final mobilization orders to the 253rd members.

A different world!

Shower time Saudi-style.

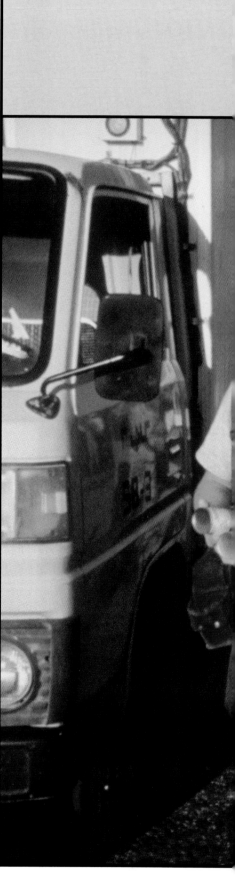

Moving across the Saudi desert.

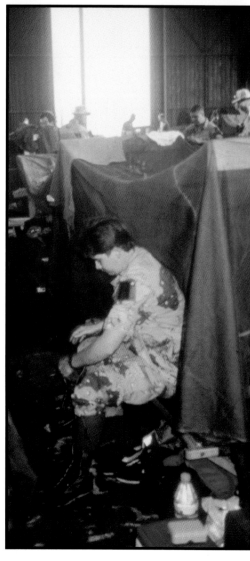

Close quarters left no room for secrets.

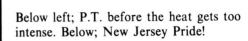

Washday Saudi-style.

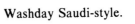

Below left; P.T. before the heat gets too intense. Below; New Jersey Pride!

Conditions did not allow for privacy.

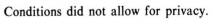

Dave Moyer & Friend

Getting ready to move out

Briefings in the open air

Gotta get all the sand out!

253rd Mission Report

On February 22nd, the company entered Iraq and began their part in the left flank encirclement of the Republican Guard, referred by General Schwarzkoph as the "Hail Mary Play". Their movement north brought them 150 miles into Iraq before a right turn towards Kuwait as a blocking force against the Republican Guard.

The clean-up provided various missions, including transport of prisoners, soldiers and supplies, back to Saudi Arabia. The 253rd was also used in transporting soldiers of the 82nd Airborne and 7th Corps to various airports on their journey home.

While in-country, the 253rd logged 834,962 mission miles and 289,000 administrative miles with only 2 accidents. They also carried 985.6 tons of cargo and 79,966 passengers.

After sanitizing their trucks, the 253rd finally left Saudi Arabia on May 27th. They arrived at Philadelphia International Airport on Tuesday, May 28th at 6:50 am and were reunited with their families and friends at Fort Dix a few hours later.

SGT Julio washing truck "Champion Maine"

(left to right) SPC Horn, SPC Kaelin, SPC Blood, SSg Longo "Taking Five Inside Iraq"

Captured equipment examined by SSG Calkins on 253rd Tractor trailer.

A ghost!?!?!

SGT Rondon on Road Block

SSG Longo, SSG Sippel, & SPC Horn deep inside Iraq

(middle right) 253rd area along the border

Taking the 82nd

Convoy on the side of the road . . . Saudi . . taking a much needed rest

Murdock & Spallina at TAA late February

Oil well Fires

ying the Flag in Iraq

Our war trophy for CMCH Armory

Singing Christmas Carols

You found me! (SPC Merkel)

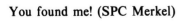

Carlos and Friends

SSG Calkins repairing starter on a 932-A2 5-ton

SFC Vey outside Rafkasa

Taking a break from sanitizing the trucks

Nice Sandstorm!!!

R & R in Barain

"Hitting the slopes?"

Moyer in the Desert Cooking Dinner

Packages from home!

Sand Bag Hotel, Camp Moody at KKMA, Saudi Arabia

(below) SPC Wuerker in MOPP level 1 sits at welcome sign to Kuwait. (left) "A Room with a View"

KFC - Riyadh

ike Vey's "Christmas in Saudi"

Waiting for a street car?

Exit 7 NJ Turnpike?

It's Lunch!

Col. F. Grutzmaester presenting Letters of Appreciation to SSG Hollino & SGT Guilins

SSG Sippel with French-made chemical detection vehicle

Vanya Bailey coming out of Iraq

Taking the 82nd to a "go" position

253rd Transportation Company
Homecoming

"I give you back your heroes", MG Vito Morgano

Glad to be home

Horn presenting guidon to MG Morgano upon
ving on U.S. soil, Philadelphia, PA.

Sean Gautier greeted by his Mother, Jennifer, at
homecoming, Ft. Dix.

3rd marching home at Ft. Dix

"Welcome Home Mom", SGT Crouse with Ben & Kelly being interviewed at homecoming.

"Honey, I'm Home!"

SPC Horn waiting to march onto field at Ft. Dix (above) SGT Veronica Muller reading paper she missed while in Saudi (right)

253rd

Cape May County awaits their heroes

SGT "Pete" Szotak's family awaits his arrival

CPT Errickson with Karen (wife) and children Daniel and Morgan

VVA Color Guard, Local 228, Welcomes home 253rd at Ft. Dix

SPC Gautier and Ariel Hemphill at homecoming

Members of SSG Sippel's family awaiting his arrival in Cape May

CH Armory Homecoming . . . We're proud of our men.

nam Veterans are part of the homecoming

1LT Sheretta with family members

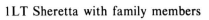

SPC Palmeria Welcomed home

CMCH Homecoming

BG Fruscione embracing a soldier

SPC Wuerker (left) SGT Gaskill enjoyin
the fire truck parade home entering
CMCH on the G.S. Parkway

etnam Veterans of America Color Guard
al 228

Homecoming CMCH . . SPC Gautier,
SPC Williams and Friend

Heroes ride fire truck to their home
armory

e're Baaaaaaaack! says SGT Roseanne Polini

Ruth Burroughs, mother of SGT Gaskill,
giving "Welcome Home Our Children"
speech at homecoming.

177th Fighter Interceptor Group

Three people from the 177th nsolidated Aircraft Maintenance uadron, Explosive Ordinance sposal Section, were activated on 2 bruary 1991. Two people were sent Bergstrom AFB, Tx and one was t to Luke AFB, Az. Why they were tivated was to provide needed ackfill" assistance to the depleted plosive Ordinance Disposal Sections. me of their duties were working the mbing ranges clearances for exploded ordinance and provided U. Secret Service support. All three ople have returned to the 177th FIG. In support of Operation Desert orm, thirteen people from the 177th curity Police Flight were activated 2 February 1991. They remained on me station to augment the existing curity Police personnel to support e increased security posture. All rteen people have been demobilized. Nine people from the 177th RMS ansportation Section were activated d sent to Seymour Johnson AFB, C. While stationed there, they ovided needed "backfill" assistance the Vehicle Operations Section as ivers of general purpose vehicles. dditionally, they assisted in the areas vehicle maintenance, working on fueling vehicles, fire trucks and the -loader, which loads C-5 pallets. The urs of duty involved long hours and certainty of schedules. All nine ople have been demobilized.

In support of Operation Desert Storm, a nine person team from the Food Service Section, 177th Services Flight were deployed to Langley AFB, Virginia which is home to the 1st Tactical Air Wing. While stationed in Virginia, some served in the base flight line kitchen while other members of the contingent of food service personnel provided assistance in billeting and other areas of base services. When the 177th members arrived in Virginia, the flight line dining area was serving 500-600 people a day which eventually increased to 800 people a day. While they generally worked a standard shift, the large contingencies of troops required them to be flexible to support the troops. The spirit of dedication on part of the 177th FIG Food Service personnel shone through day after day.

The 177th USAF Clinic deployed to USAF Medical Center, Keesler AFB, MS during the period 8 February 1991 to 22 March 1991 due to being activated for Operation Desert Storm. A total of twenty-five Clinic personnel were deployed. The primary purpose of this deployment was a partial mobilization to provide contingency support and backfill personnel deployed from USAFMC Keesler.

Clinic personnel were integrated into various sections within the hospital, to include Patient Affairs, Admissions, Orderly Room, Outpatient Records,

Emergency Room, Primary Care Clinic, Radiology, Bioenvironmental, Environmental Health, Laboratory, Optometry, Flight Medicine, Dental, and various nursing wards (i. e., Oncology, Intensive Care).

177th Fighter Interceptor Group

177FIG Desert Storm Participants

SPF

SSGT CHRISTOPHER A. MOZITIS
SSGT JEROME T. STAQUET
SGT JOHN C. CATHERINE
SGT JOHN C. WATSON
SRA DAVID DIAZ
SRA JOLEEN P. PETERSON
A1C MARY M. CONNELLY
A1C SHANE DALY
SRA DAVID M. HERITAGE
A1C WILLIAM HANKINS JR.
A1C JOSEPH B. MAY
AMN CHARLES J. CARUSO
AMN DARREN J. MARINO

RMS (TRANSPORTATION)

TSGT STEVE F. FERNANDEZ
TSGT HAROLD M. IRELAND
TSGT DANIEL P. KERNS
TSGT WILLIAM D. LAW
TSGT DENNIS M. MCREYNOLDS
TSGT JAMES H. NORCROSS
TSGT STEVE RIVERA
SSGT MARIO SERRANODEJESUS
SSGT EDWARD E. WHITLAND JR.

CES (FIRE DEPARTMENT)

MSGT DOMINICK P. GALIONE

MSGT WILLIAM P. MOORE JR.
TSGT LESLIE W. ALLEN
TSGT RICHARD J. DEALY III
TSGT JOHN J. DUFFY
TSGT JAMES P. HANNON SR.
TSGT JOHN W. HANNUM
SSGT JAMES T. BIRD
SSGT MICHAEL T. HARRY
SSGT JEFFREY J. SILAGY
SSGT ROBERT V. WUTTKE
SGT SAMMY B. YATES

VOLUNTARY PARTICIPANTS

CMSGT EDWARD W. WOLBERT
MSGT PETER P. SINKO

CLINIC

COL STANLEY C. KELLEY
LTCOL BARBARA A. LOGAN
MAJOR LADISLAO M. AGUILA
MAJOR WAYNE S. CASSEDY
LTCOL VALDIS JURKA
CAPT BARBARA A. BURROWS
MAJOR DANIEL J. CIECHANOWSKI
CAPT SHEILA A. FITZGERALD
1LT GERALD J. IULIUCCI
1LT MARTIN S. MANNO
TSGT TERESA

CASSADY
TSGT JOSEPH F. CIRILLO
TSGT HAROLD R. COX JR.
TSGT DIANNA D. GUGLIOTTA
TSGT KIM KELLY
TSGT ARTHUR H. ST. JOHN
TSGT SILAS A. LAKE JR.
TSGT GRANT S. BEAMER
SSGT KENNETH E. BRENT
SSGT DIANE E. CARNEY
SSGT F. HETZEL
SSGT KENNETH M. MCHALE
SRA VICKY L. TIGHE
AMN DREAMA A. CHANNELS
AMN JENNIFER M. PERKINS

FIG

TSGT EDWARD A. DITORO

CAM (EOD)

SSGT JEFF C. KWILINSKI

TSGT WILLIAM T. MORGAN III
SSGT DANIEL P. DUFFY

SVF (FOOD SERVICE)

TSGT WILLIAM A. DAYTON
TSGT RICHARD A. JENNI
TSGT ANTHONY J. PADULA
SSGT JOSEPH M. AMICI
SSGT CALVIN M. BARTECHKO
SSGT DAVID N. GOLDBERG
SSGT WILLIAM G. JOSEPH
SSGT DANIEL L. LASH
SSGT ROBERT F. YOUNG JR.

ission Report Cont'd

or the unit's Chaplain's Assistant, urday of February UTA was truly a of change. Ed DiToro began the drill ning as a SSgt and ended the day as a t. He also received orders effective 9 ruary to be on station in Saudi Arabia Saturday, 16 February. TSgt DiToro nediately proceeded to attend to a series dministrative matters before heading to firing range to qualify in the M-16. further training, highly accelerated due he timing of events, included chemical fare training which was conducted at Guire AFB.

Sgt DiToro was situated at an air base central Saudi Arabia which was home to omposite wing that played a very key e in the air war against Iraq. There e a group of chaplains and chaplain stants who hail from all over the ntry. As the NCOIC (called Chief of apel Support Activities - CCSA), Ed s responsible for coordinating almost 30 kly religious services in addition to le Studies, AA meetings, and eployment/reunion briefings. In addition his busy schedule, TSgt DiToro's chapel ff was recently selected by HDQTRS, wn as USCENTAF, to provide a nistry to a small, but brave contingent of S. Air Force personnel at the Kuwait ernational Airport. Two chaplains and gt DiToro go there every week for two ys and provide religious services and nseling to about 125 people. TSgt

DiToro returned to the 177th FIG on 13 July 1991.

During the July UTA, the 177th FIG focused their attention on two aspects of Air National Guard membership which are the essence of the Guard experience— service and family.

Nearly all of the unit members who were mobilized during Desert Shield/Storm have returned to the 177th and to their families. Most of them served at various Air Force bases in the United States as replacements for active duty personnel sent to the Persian Gulf theater of operations, and one individual to the region. Most of the mobilized people had very short notice of their call-up and little time to tend to their professional and personal affairs before departing to their active duty assignments. They experienced the turmoil that readiness mission occasionally requires.

The 177 FIG Desert Storm Homecoming Picnic afforded the 177th FIG to proudly welcome these men and women back to the unit and at the same time extend gratitude to their families for their support during the mobilization period.

Operation Desert Shield has commanded world attention since the fateful invasion date of August 2, 1990. Active duty, National Guard and Reserve components have responded in strength in terms of both activations and volunteers to units being deployed both stateside and to the

Persian Gulf region. The spirit of cooperation and top flight professionalism which have always been the hallmarks of the 177th FIG was once again fully demonstrated as unit members assisted sister units during this time of crisis and challenge.

Desert Shield came home to the 177th when twelve fire Fighters were ordered to active duty. They were stationed in Eglin AFB, Florida for a 90 day or more period which began on 9 December 1990. This call-up accounts for 25% of the fire fighters, who, as part of the Civil Engineering Squadron, protects the Group's personnel and equipment from the danger of conflagration.

The Fire Fighters had received word about a month before that such an activation might occur. The official word was not received, however, until 6 December 1990. The members had been preparing since that time, but there was still a feeling that there might be two weeks leeway before departure. That leeway translated into four days and caused the celebration of some early and abbreviated Christmas festivities. This included gift exchanges and traditional dinners the night following the call-up.

On 7 December, the fire fighters went over last minute paperwork and began packing for the trip south. Eglin is located near Fort Walton Beach in the Florida panhandle.

Clinic personnel receiving their mobilization briefing.

Transportation personnel during outprocessing.

Brig. Gen. Taylor talking to the transportation people.

Col. Griffin talking to the transportation people.

Fire Department working on a truck.

Col. Tom Griffin and TSgt Ed Ditord at the 177th FIG Desert Storm Homecoming Picnic.

Colonel Stan Kelley, 177 USAF Clinic Commander, recognizes his personnel at Keesler AFB for their fine work during Desert Storm.

Some 177th personnel being honored at the Desert Storm Homecoming Picnic Commander's call.

(right) Annemarie Cunningham addresses 177
FIG families at the Family Support Workshop.
(far right) LTC Elizabeth Yull

Cpt. Budd Springer addresses
Family Support Workshop.

Wives of some of 177th FIG personnel

177 CES Fire Dept. Training.

Some of the 177 CES Fire Dept. personnel.

TSgt Ed Ditoro, Chaplain's Assistant in Kuwait

Transportation people receiving mobilization briefing.

177th USAF Clinic
Personnel at Keesler AFB.
Col. Stan Kelley (in flight
suit) Clinic Commander

177th

The mission of the 144th Supply Company (HVMAT) (GS) during Operation Desert Shield/Storm/Farewell was both interesting and tasking, starting with the mobilization of the unit to the redeployment plans of late June early July 1991.

The mobilization process started with the 144th Supply Company being activated on 21 November 1990 and reporting to Fort Dix, New Jersey on 25 November 1990. After successfully completing processing for

overseas replacement (or POR) processing, the unit started completing basic soldier skills training, such as weapons qualification, chemical protection and military occupational skills training.

The unit then deployed to the southwest Asia theater of operations (Saudi Arabia). We were housed in a condominium complex in a town called Khobar. Although the condos were not furnished the living conditions were not that bad. We slept on cots in sleeping bags and had regular bathrooms to use with running water. During our stay in Khobar we

were not in any direct danger of attack. Oh, yes, we did have to contend with the nightly Scud missile attacks but after the first few days this became more of a joke than a real threat. After spending about 1 month in Khobar and listening to the air war on the radio and television (yes, some of us had TV) the unit deployed to a military installation called King Khalid Military City or KKMC for short.

At KKMC the unit was housed in tents, living out in the desert. Most of the unit was employed in the following manner:

144th Supply Company

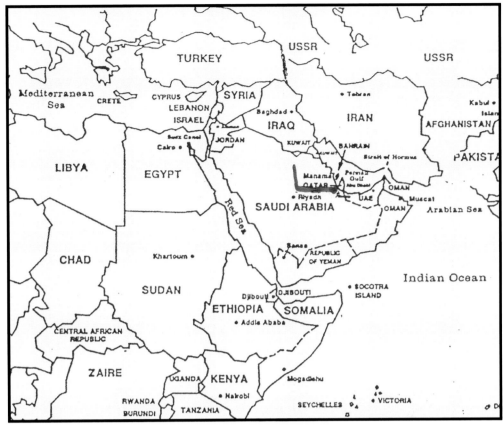

Supply Operations Office - Basically ran the operation in regard to the inventory control for the items that we stored.

Processing Platoon - Processed work orders for the equipment stored by the equipment storage platoon. Also was tasked for the storage of a tactical petroleum tankfarm and the receipt and storage of equipment from the 3rd Armor Division that was to be left in Saudi Arabia at a temporary storage location.

Equipment Storage Platoon - Tasked with the storage of damaged American equipment (tanks, armored personnel carriers, etc). Some of this material was damaged during the ground offensive, however, most was unserviceable due to engines failing or transmissions breaking and not being able to repair them on the battlefield.

Fortification & Construction Storage Platoon - This platoon had the most interesting job of all. They were responsible for the storage of captured enemy equipment. This consisted of items from AK-47 rifles to T-72 tanks that were captured during the conflict.

On the 15th of June 1991 the 144th Supply Company assumed the missions of the 1012th General Support Company and the 165th Supply Company.

The missions of these two units were as follows:

1012th General Supply Company - Responsible for storage of Class I (food or subsistence items), Class II (clothing), Class IIIP (petroleum products, packaged)

165th Supply Company - Responsible for the storage of Class IV (construction items) and Class VII (wheeled vehicles).

In addition to the above stated missions this unit also supported the following details

PX - This is like a small department store or grocery store.

Laundry - This is the place where all or most of the soldiers have their clothing cleaned.

Telephone Center - Enabling all soldiers to be able to phone home.

Central Issue Facility - This is the place that issues all clothing and office supplies to units.

Guard Duty - This duty was performed at Khobar and was done in both a stationary position and a walking patrol.

Consolidated Dining Facility - The location where most of KKMC went to eat meals.

So as you can see the 144th Supply Company was very busy with a wide variety of interesting missions. We had our times when tempers flared, when homesickness set in and our spirits were down. All of us shared our home news, newspapers and other things from home, anything to remind us of New Jersey. However, when duty called, the 144th Supply Company stood proudly and pulled together to **get the job done.**

The 144th
Commander - Cpt. James J. Casalunova

Sgt. Major - 1SG. William F. Cloer Jr.

ALEXANDER, TERRY
ALLEN, TSG. LESLIE W.
ALSTON, SGT. MILDRED
BARTHOLOMEW, PV2. ROBERT
BATES, SPC. JANINE A.
BELL, ERIC L.
BIRD, SSG. JAMES T.
BLAND, PV2 TRACY
BRAUN, SPC. DANIEL
BRAXTON, PFC. DON J.
BROWN, PFC. WILLIAM A.
BRUNZO, SGT. LINDA L.
BULL, SPC. WILSON A.
BURGESS, SPC. JASON
CADE, WILLIAM, JR.
CAIN, SPC. STACY L
CALABRIA, CW3 MATTHEW C.
CALDWELL, SGT. CAROLYN A.
CARTER, SPC. LISA M.
CARTER, 2LT LESLIE T.
CASALUNOVA, CPT. JAMES J.
CASANOVA, SGT. RAYMOND
CHAVERS, PFC. JERRY
CHIRICO, SGT. VICTOR
CLOER, 1SG. WILLIAM F., JR.
COOK, SSG. DARRYL V.
CORCINO, SGT. RIVERA B.
CROSKEY, SPC. MICHAEL
CRUZ, SPC. WILBERT
CUNNINGHAM, SSG. GRANT, JR.
DAVIS, SGT. DONALD L., III
DEALY, RICHARD J.
DEHOYOS, PV2 WILFREDO
DEWITT, RICHARD D.
DIGUGLIELMO, SGT. BART A.
DIGUGLIELMO, BILL A.
DONOVAN, PFC. LEE S.
DOWE, PVC. PATRICE A.
DOYLE, RAYMOND
DUDA, SGT. JAMES J.
DUFFY, SSG. JOHN J.
DUNLAP, DEBORAH L.
EASTER, NICOLA
ELLIS, SSG. JOSEPH G.
FEASTER, PV2 ANTHONY P.
FINCH, SPC. MICHAEL
FINNEY, SPC. PHILIP A.
FREW, SPC. DAVID
GARCIA, FRANKLIN M.
GIANONNE, SGT. BENITO
GOTTFRIED, PV2. JOHN W.
GOYCO, SPC. JULIO E.
GREENLEE, SGT. KENNETH
HAGEN, SSG. NILS K., JR.
HAGEN, SGT. WILLIAM J.
HALL, SGT. ANDREW, III

HAND, SPC. BARRY E.
HANS, PFC. STEVEN N.
HARPER, SGT. JOHN C.
HARRISON, SPC. HOWARD K.
HAWN, SGT. JOSEPH H., SR.
HELLIWELL, CHARLES E.
HERNANDEZ, SSG. GILBERTO
HINCHMAN, SGT. DOUGLAS
HUELAS, PV1 ANNE L.
IBAY, SPC. ELIAS
JACKSON, PV1 JOHNNIE O.
JENNINGS, SPC. LAWRENCE
JOHNSON, SPC. BRIAN L.
JOHNSTON, SGT. PUAL A.
JOYCE, SSG. STEPHEN M.
KARPIAK, SPC. CHARLES E.
KEATING, CW2 RICHARD J.
KEPPEN, SPC. KARL N.
KILBY, SSG. RONALD P.
KIRBY, SGT. EUGENE, JR.
KIRBY, SGT. RONALD M.
KLAUDI, SGT. JOSEPH E.
KOCH, SGT. JEFFREY J.
KUEHNER, PFC. LISA M.
LAFRANCE, PFC. DADMA MM.
LANE, SPC. WILLIAM
LANGHEIM, SGT. HARRY E., JR.
LAZARUS, BERL
LELLO, SGT. ANGELO R.
LENT, PFC. JEFFREY M.
LEON, SPC. JUAN J.
LEWIS, SPC. MARCUS W.
MACON, SGT. SANDRA L.
MADDOX, SSG. MELVIN H.
MARSHALL, PV2 JASON T.
MARSHALL, SHERYL A.
MARTINEZ, SGT. VALAQUEZ A.
MARTINEZ, JULIO A.
MAYFIELD, PV2. TORRES W.
MC CLEARY, 1LT. DENISE K.
MC BRIDE, SGT. FRANK, JR.
MC KENZIE, SSG. THOMAS
MC NAIR, SGT. ELWELL
MINCEY, SPC. HILTON, III
MOREY, PV1 DENNIS P.
MUNFORD, SGT. JOHN A., JR.
MURDOCK, SPC. ROBERT D.
NEWKIRK, SPC. TANYA MM.
NICHOLS, SGT. PAUL
NIEVES, SPC. JOHNNY
OBRIEN, SPC. JOHN S.
OLIVER, ROBERT
OMROD, SPC. HAROLD J.
ORIENTE, PV2 ANTHONY W.
PACHECO, SPC. JOSE L.
PAGAN, SGT. JOSE M.

PALMER, 1LT. CARL A.
PANZERA, SPC. MARK
PARAMORE, LESTER A.
PEARSON, SPC. DAVID E., JR.
PEDRICK, SGT. RALPH
PEREZ, PV1. THOMAS
PEREZ, SPC. RODOLFO
PETTIT, PFC. BRUCE W.
PORTER, SPC. DONALD D.
PORTER, SGT. KENNETH J.
POWELL, SSG. DAVID A.
QUINN, SPC. DONALD L., JR.
RAMIREZ, SPC. ARTURO
RAMOS, SPC. ERROL J.
RIVERA, SGT. SANTIAGO E.
RODRIGUEZ, SPC. BERNICE V.
RODRIGUEZ, SGT. ROBERT
RODRIGUEZ, SPC. DANIEL V.
RODRIGUEZ, SSG. MICHAEL
ROSARIO, SSG. RUBIN
ROWELL, SGT. BARRY D.
RYKER, SGT. DALE A.
SANTIAGO, EUGENIO
SANTIAGO, SGT. CARMEN L.
SAWYER, SPC. KEVIN D.
SCOTT, MARCO A.
SEGUI, SGT. JAVIER
SERRANO, SSG. ED A.
SETTLE, JOSEPH T.
SEVERINO, PFC. JUAN A.
SHEPHERD, SFC. JOHN C., JR.
SILVA, PV2 ROBERTO
SIMMS, 1LT. JOHN W.
SNYDER, SGT. BONNIE
SOCKWELL, SPC. LEAMY L.
SPINA, SGT. PATRICK J.
STEFFA, SGT. DONALD D., JR.
STEINKE, SPC. PETER
STEVENSON, SPC. DARRYL
SUPER, CW2 ERNEST C.
SWEENEY, SGT: COLLEEN
TAYLOR, SSG. EDMOND J.
THOMPSON, SPC. SHARON T.
TRAMONTANA, PFC. JUDITH A.
VALEZ, ANGEL
VANDERVORT, SPC. JOSEPH F.
WAY, SPC. RICHARD E.
WESP, SGT. WILLIAM
WESTERVELT, SGT. EDWARD J.
WHITE, SPC. SERRENIA
WILLIAMS, PFC. EVA M.
WILLIAMS, SPC. CHARLES E.
WILLIAMSON, MARCUS A.
YOUNG, PFC. TYRONE A.
ZITZMAN, SGT. FRANK

144th loading up at the Ft. Dix Armory.

The 144th at Ft. Dix.

Family goodbyes at Hammonton.

144th farewell at Hammonton.

Some engagements were shortened. SGT. James J. Duda and his new wife, Danielle, on his wedding day, 11/27/90, at Ft. Dix.

(below) Ft. Dix, Nov. 90.   Juan Leon prepares to leave.

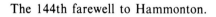

The 144th farewell to Hammonton.

At Fort Dix. Even the floor is better than those army cots.

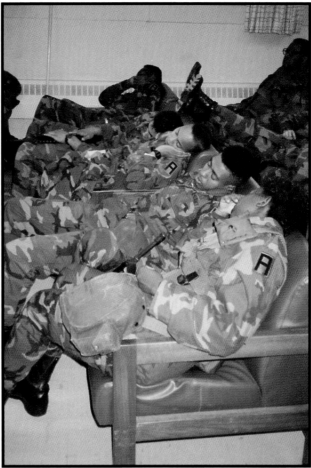

(above right) The
144th at Ft. Dix
. . . Hurry up
and wait!
(above left) Now it's
a go . . . Make way!

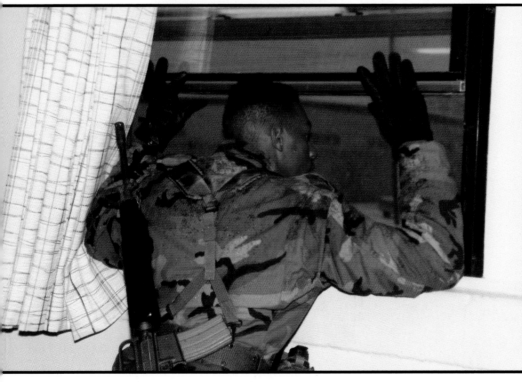

the Ft. Dix Armory. The situation becomes serious.

The 144th good to go!

The 144th in-country. SGT. Benito Gianone. Love is where you find it!

) The 144th at the Ft. Dix Armory.
her Nature gets into the picture.

The 144th stopover in Germany.

An All-American Bar-b-Que

G. John Shepherd, SPC. Lisa Keuhner,
nald Davis, SGT. Anthony Gianone.

In-Country. Maid's day off!

Is this how they measured how much space
they get?

Card-playing passes the hours.

Steffa, Hanns, Oriente, and Bartholomew.

Bruce Pettit, Peter Steinke, Sandra Macon, Mildred Austin, Charles Karpiak, and Nicole Eastar

El Khobar Moving day! This certainly
beats the stairs.

Ken Porter. "But I like this music."

"This is a what?"

El Khobar Hilton. Mincey,
Jennings, Bull, Valez,
Bartholomew.

"Shep's Junk Yard."

Cpt. James Casalunova, SSG. John
Shepherd, 1SG William Cloer, 1LT. John
Simms at Command Post.

3rd Platoon at morning formation.

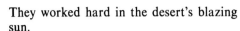
Eve Williams takes a rest where and when she can in Saudi.

They worked hard in the desert's blazing sun.

John Harper in an 88 Recovery Vehicle.

Burning the "Honey Pots."

SFC John C. Shepherd, Jr. armed in the desert.

PFC. Nick Morgan and Sgt. Beni Giannone lift equipment to check out the sand damage.

Sgt. Colleen Sweeney

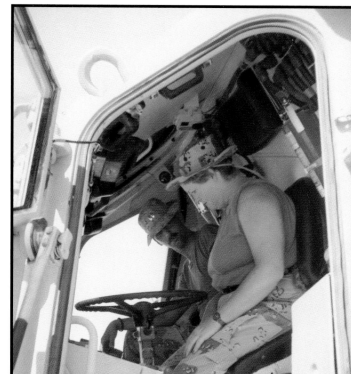

SSG Dale Ryker, "Desert Cowboy"

Equipment must be moved. Even that with Playboy Bunnies on it.

Eddie and the 144th Mascot, "Scud."

Showers at KKMC.

144th

Obstructions in the desert.

Sgt. Anthony Gagliardi and Cpt. James
Casalunova setting up the kitchen.

Chow time for the guys from the 2nd
Platoon, KKMC.

Touches from New Jersey. Note the pine cone and boughs in the upper left of the picture.

SSG. John A. Mumford checks out captured equipment.

Member of the 144th looks like Moses crossing the desert.

Sgt. Colleen Sweeney poses by sign with familiar names at a 253rd campsite.

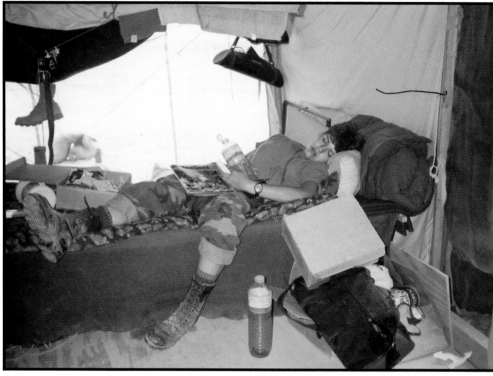

Home Sweet Home! Home is where you make it. As long as there is water.

Not all of the work of war is destruction. Greenlea, Martinez, Ramos, and Serrano prepare building materials.

Jersey Ra

...tting up some homey touches in the ...sert.

Construction ingenuity is shown in backboard and stand erected in desert.

...action in the desert.

Sgt. John Shepherd getting ready to test the food.

Easter Sunday Service.
Below; Voices are raised at the Easter Sunday Service (KKMC)

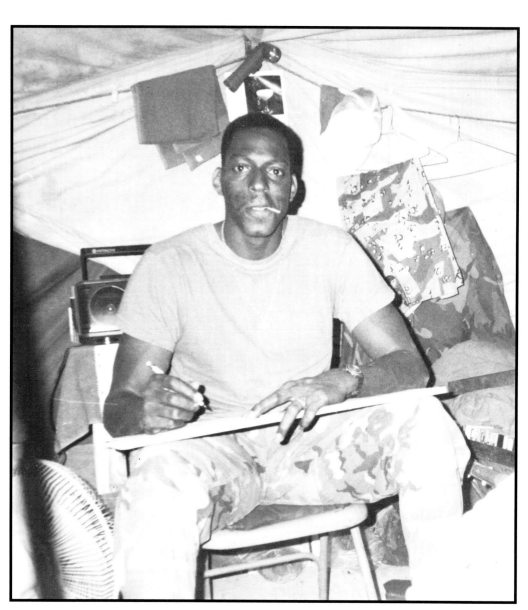

Writing helped pass the time and kept open the links to home.

W. DeGugliamo, Terry Alexander, Frank Garcia, Daniel Brown, John Harper, and Gilbert Hernandez in the desert.

Coffee break relieves the tension of war.

The pressures of combat show in the face of Johnny Nieves.

Prepared to go! Lt. Leslie Carter, Anthony Franter, Terry Alexander, John Blue.

The 144th in FEST tent. Advance group to KKMC.

(left to right) MAJ Maryellen Yacka, 2LT Lynn Molinar, MAJ Roseanne Menth, 1LT Carol Rippel, 2LT Patricia Baylog, 1LT Deborah Pere, Col. Elizabeth Koster (Commander), CPT Judy Applegate, CPT June Stewart, 2LT Kathy Walsh, CPT Debbie Hogrefe and MAJ Kathy Morrissey

213th Health Service Liasion Detachment

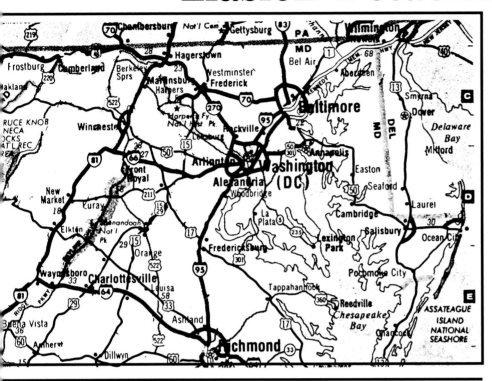

On Saturday, 26 January 1991 the nurses of the 213th reported to the New Jersey Military Academy Sea Girt, New Jersey for preparation for mobilization.

At 1300 hours MG Morgano met with the nurses and informed them that they would be going to report to Walter Reed Army Medical Center.

On 1 February 1991 the nurses again reported to Sea Girt for more administrative work and another meeting with MG Morgano. They were told that Walter Reed was the mobilization station and there was no guarantee that we would stay there.

We reported to Walter Reed and received our assignments. MAJ Morrissey, 1LT Pere, 1LT Walsh and 1LT Rippel were assigned to the Operating Room. LT Molinaro was assigned to the Emergency Room. MAJ Menth and CPT Applegate were assigned to a Psychiatric Unit. CPT Stewart and CPT Hogrefe were assigned to Medical Units. MAJ Yacka was assigned to a Surgical Unit. 1LT Baylog was assigned to Intensive Care. COL Koster was assigned to the Staff Development Section.

Patients from Saudi Arabia were arriving even before the ground war started. There were illnesses and injuries to be expected with the massive numbers of troops deployed in the Gulf and the patients would arrive at all hours of the day or night still in their desert uniforms, tired and in need of a shower, something to eat and a comfortable bed. Most of the patients were routed from Saudi Arabia through Germany and then to Walter Reed.

It wasn't long after the scud attack that the casualties began arriving at Walter Reed. The injuries were quite severe on many of the patients and many of them were also very young. They were cared for by nurses in the operating room and then on the floors. Many of the nurses of the 213th had an opportunity to meet them and talk to them about their experiences and give them the best care possible.

For those soldiers who were injured in the Gulf, their medical care was expertly handled from the front lines to the United States. The nurses from the 213th drew from their varied civilian backgrounds and experience to give the patients the care they deserved. More than one patient commented on how pleasant and professional the reserve medical personnel were. A number of the casualties were reservists themselves. It was truly a unique situation. A group of civilian citizen soldiers were part of the active army in one of the most rapid mobilizations in history.

1LT Baylog personally took care of one POW for several days in the Intensive Care Unit giving him both physical care and emotional support.

The active duty tour ended officially on 2 April 1991. Once again, the HSLD, 213th Medical Brigade from New Jersey was part of the New Jersey Army National Guard.

MAJ Menth during in-
processing

1LT Baylog being fitted
M17 A1 Gas Mask

213th In-Processing

More In-Processing

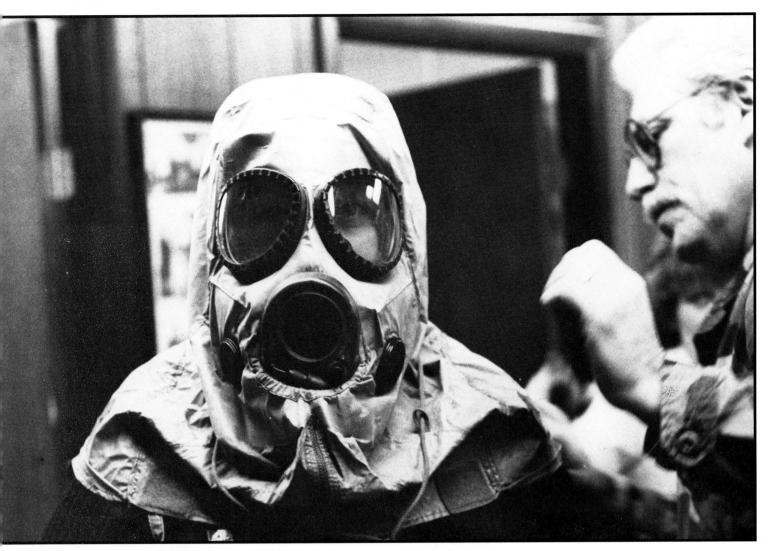

and still More In-Processing

d More In-Processing

1LT Rippel and Children at Farewell

Flag at farewell

Family and Friends during farewell
ceremony

CPT Stewart & 1LT Walsh with Joan
Haberle, NJ Secy. of State

Chaplain Joann Martindale at farewell

Emotions run high at farewell . . Everyone needed a
hug!

MG Vito Morgano with 1LT Baylor and 1LT Pere

A picture is worth a thousand words

Col. Koster presenting Cpt. Hogrefe a saber for dedication in ensuring the units readiness for active duty.

Some more In-Processing

LT Pere gets a farewell hug from Col. Sally O'Hare, Chief Nurse of the NJ National Guard. Looking on are Deputy Commissioner Barnard, Veterans Division and Brig. Gen. Preston Taylor, Deputy Adjutant General of New Jersey

108th Tactical Fighter Wing

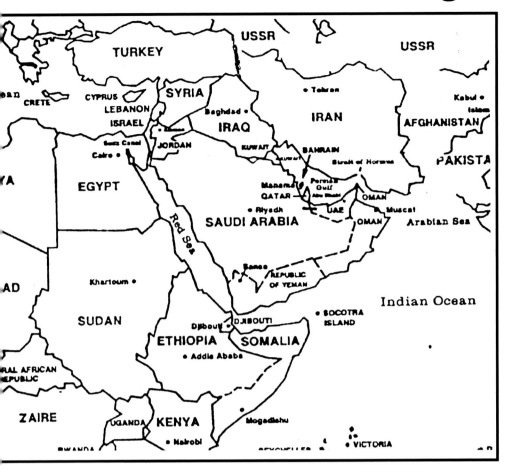

The 108 TFW contributed to the success of operations in Southwest Asia by providing the following support.

DESERT SHIELD

a. Colonel Dutko (DCR) received a phone call early on 6 August 1990, enacting partial alert of Funds Management, Base Supply and the Comptroller functions to support Operation Desert Shield. Quick and effective response ensured that two KC-135s and their aircrews were ready to deploy by 0800 hours that day. The full-time Resources Management Squadron (RMS) supported the 170 Air Refueling Group during the entire conflict.

b. The 108 TAC Clinic's scheduled overseas annual training in Sep 90 was rescheduled by the National Guard Bureau. Approximately 45 personnel deployed to Shaw AFB, S.C. to backfill for active duty personnel deployed to Southwest Asia. The clinic's deployment lasted two weeks. A flight medical technician remained at Shaw for six months.

c. Nine members of the 108 Consolidated Aircraft Maintenance Squadron (CAMS) supported the US Army at the Army Depot in Bayonne, N.J.

during October 1990. They saved several hundred thousand dollars by repainting sixty M-1A1 Abrams main battle tanks in desert camouflage colors.

d. MSgt Bernard Unterkoefler (108 RMS) was TDY to Forbes ANG Base in Kansas during November 1990 to support Desert Shield Central. He helped develop a deployed manning document and assisted schedule personnel and aircraft to Saudi Arabia.

2. DESERT STORM

a. From January 12 to March 1, 1991, the 108 TFW supported eight F-4G (Wild Weasel) from the 35 TFW, George AFB, CA., four RF-4C aircraft from the 67 TRW, Bergstrom AFB, TX, and several F-4Es from the 3TFW, Clark AB, the Philippines, which were enroute to Southwest Asia. These aircraft were staged at McGuire and then launched to Saudi Arabia.

(1) Wing operations personnel operated a 24-hour command post, developed training schedules, processed over 50 aircrews, flew training missions with the transient aircrews to maintain mission readiness status, established

Mission Report Cont'd.

refueling schedules and coordinated range operations.

(2) 108 CAMS personnel maintained these transient aircraft around the clock to ensure they were ready to deploy overseas on a moments notice.

(3) 108 RMS personnel provided transient aircraft and aircrews with transportation, fuel, logistics and supply support.

b. The 108 Mission Support Squadron's Services Section provided four volunteers for 90 days to work at the McGuire AFB Falcon Dining Hall to

support increased Main Base work schedules, etc.

MSgt Richard Kulesa, 108 MSS Services Section, and TSgt Joseph Schab, 108 Security Police Flight, were TDY to the National Guard Bureau at Andrews AFB from January thru July and 2 Jan to 4 May 1991, respectively. They manned the Air Guard's command post operation to provide activation notices and points of contact for either Services/Civil Engineer or Security Police guardsmen who were deploying.

The 108 TAC Clinic sent MSgt Debra

Baker, an opometry technician, to McDill AFB, Fl., for thirty days. Captain Andrew Savicky, a clinical psychologist was deployed to Luke AFB, AZ., for 30 days. Senior Airm Scott Leary, a flight medical technician, and Israel Gonzalez, a medical services technician, were deployed to Shaw AFB, S.C. for ove 1/2 months.

108th Tactical Fighter Wing

108th CAM
PAINT ARMY
M1A1 TANKS FOR
DESERT SHIELD

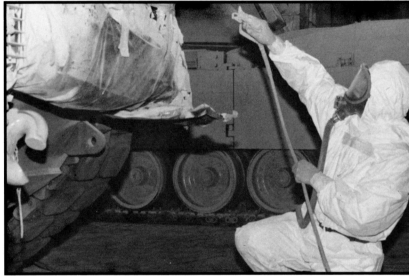

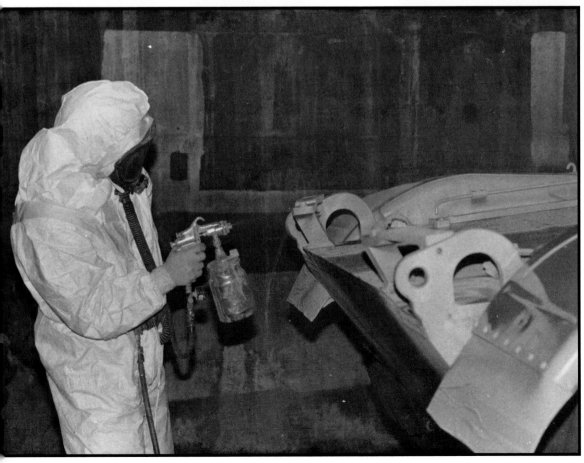

-G Wild Weasel prepped for SWA by 108th

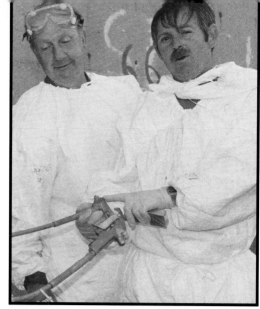

108th

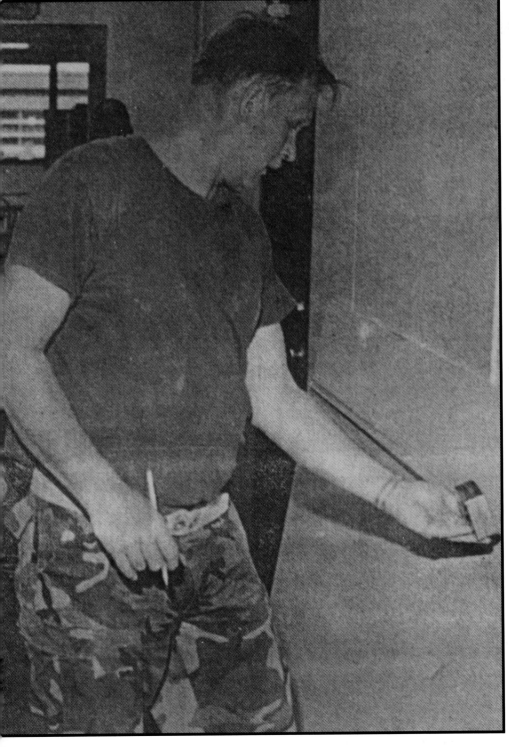

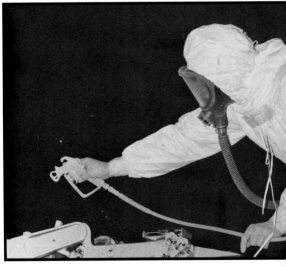

MEMORIES OF A SOLDIER

**Watercolors done in-country by J. Stagg
and letters home from the soldiers of
the New Jersey National Guard.**

Dear Family   FEB 23RD, 91   ④

    How is everyone? Good I hope
I finally hit the desert a few
days ago. Let me tell you as glad
as I was to get here I'm ready
to come home.

    Let me tell you exactly what is
going on here. Yesterday the ground
war began. And you could see planes
taking off one after another after
another. Going to fly a bombing
mission in Iraq. We also had
a few scud missles but they
all went towards Isreal and
not us. I hope that all this will
end soon and I'm back on the
plane home.

    We have been on ACTIVE DUTY for
3 months and a few days and
May is just around the corner.
I keep saying "Lets go May" but
we might be here longer who
knows I sure don't.

Bid with all truth I miss and
love you all and I shall be home
in One piece and safe.

    Tell issa that bobby will
be home soon and he loves
and misses you.

You you all

        Love
    Robert P. Bartholomew

Prayer for Military Spouses

Eternal God,
we thank you for the significant relationships that
are such an important part of life; especially those
we share within our own families. Help us to
strengthen these relationships by our sensitivity to
each other and by our willingness to practice
patience, understanding and forgiveness within our
homes.

Give us the strength to face the daily challenges and
sacrifices that are part of the life style we experience
within the military community. May we develop a
balanced outlook on life and a deep commitment to
each other as we seek to live out our lives in
healthy interdependence. Help us to be mindful of the
significant influence we have on each other, through
the encouraging touch, the understanding smile and
the many small acts of kindness.

May we give generously of ourselves to the noble
causes that are so important to our world, our
nation and our communities. Enable us to become
totally dedicated to the sanctity of marriage and the
health of our families which serve as the foundation
of society.

We offer this prayer in gratitude for all the blessings
of the past and with hope in that which awaits us
in the future. In your name we pray. Amen.

MG Stuart E. Barstad
Chief of Chaplains
United States Air Force

Military Spouse Day 1988
Office of Family Policy & Support
Department of Defense

January 27, 1991

Dear Love

We are now at the Oasis
our new home. It's about
7 miles on Route Toyota (west)
Some road to Riyadh. My
little Valentine I love
you very much. Some
day we will be together,
just hope its quick. Very
soon Saddam will be
taken care of. Love you dearly.
By for now!
Love,
Frankie

"Crisis In Peace"

Can we beat them, is that what you ask?
My answer to that is we've already kicked ass.
Through the air we have flown like a kite.
With wishful thinking, through morning and night.

On the ground, the war had yet to begin,
for the fear seeps beyond thy skin.
The skin of a soldier who has tried their best,
They know until the job is done, there was no
rejoice in peaceful rest

There are no winners or losers at that.
Just people who remained in well-known packs.
Fighting for justice and peace at heart,
vowed to their country to never part.

Bands play for the high flying flag.
To remind those who are often quite sad.
That those who have served our country proud,
will be back . . . someday, somehow.

A thanks to our troops
on ground, water, and in air.
We want you to know, we love you and care.

With love and trust through the end.
We love you dearly,
my sweet friend.

Written By: Michele A. Ray
Age: 15

A Day in the Desert

A bead of sweat rolls down my cheek,
Along with the passing of another week.
Thoughts of friends, brothers and sisters,
Mom and Dad,
And of the life I once had.
Deserted in this barren land,
In the company of only desert sand.
M-2 burners increase intense heat,
Yet someone must cook so we can eat.
X-mas came but wasn't the same,
For we were locked into a deadly game.
We men could fight and some may die,
Tears join my sweat as my soul cries.
Mail call comes with a word from home,
No longer do I feel alone.
I remember I'm not at the end of my rope,
Concern from loved ones gives me hope.
For someday I'll be back in the air,
Heading for home and leaving my despair.

Carlos Scull
Operation Desert Storm

SPC Edward Barnes greeting Christine Gruenler

WELCOME HOME

"Be careful," "Stay safe," "I'll miss you,"
These words they used to say
When your country called you
And sent you far away

You did your very best
You went in feeling tough
Keeping those bad feelings inside
When times were a little rough

The long, hot, dragging days
And sleepless nights you spent
Thinking of all your loved ones at home
You risked your life to defend

This is my point of view
Of what I'd imagined it'd be
But only a veteran would really know
The dreams and fears they've seen

You're finally coming home
And those feelings have gone away
The Star Spangled Banner flies higher than ever
And that's the way its gonna stay

So let the bands play on
It's time to celebrate
Welcome home America
You were really great

5-31-91
CHRISTINE
GRUENLER

Samantha Beth Goldman   Date 3/21/91

Dear Sir,
            I am so happy the war is over.
I hope you will be home safely real soon. What is your
job? What is it like? And why? What is the weather
like out there?
(ﾟ_ﾟ)

            My name is Samantha Beth
Goldman. And I am nine years old. I don't no to much
about the war but I am sure glad you guys did such
a wonderful job. My whole family thanks you for helping
to protect our flag. I'm sure glad your coming home
soon. Maybe you can come to our school and tell what
it was like in the War. Take care of yourself. We are
very proud of you. By.

                            Love
                            Samantha
                            Beth
                            Goldman

Dear Mom

Just a few lines to let you know
I'm alright and still ticking as you
know were at war I won't be able
to call but if I can you'll be
the first to try to relax I'm with
20 men who know what their doing
this will probly be the last letter
until this ordeal is over Love you
give everyone a kiss for me
and I love you all.
and please don't
worry so much   Take Care
what happens happens Love you
god will take care all
of me Love always
      From yours truly

            Tony

February 1, 1991

2

Dearest Rose,

My mind is always with you honey, it is really difficult for me not to wander back to our earlier times, I surely miss everything about those times. Honey each fox hole will be safer then the next, because I want to come home to my little pumpkin! Saddam Hussein is an asshole and then nothing short of that. In the last two days his forces have been beaten by the Saudi's troops, with the help of the US Airforce. Leave Ron Midura alone honey, he finally got the new contract.

Honey, here are a few pictures that were taken by J.C. camera, add them to the album. I love you terribly, and want to be in your arms real soon. Hoping that this war is over in a few weeks.

Love always

AMANDA'S POEM

Amanda Leah, my beautiful little girl,
I would give you anything in this world.
You see, Daddy is so far from home,
A gift I can't give, so I write you this poem.
I wish you the happiest birthday of them all,
'I would like to be there, or even be able to call.
When you were small I had to part,
Ever since then I've had this empty space in my
heart.
Someday in the future when I return,
This empty space will be filled as you will soon
learn.
I long to see your cute little smiles,
For this I'd walk ten thousand miles.
A kiss and a hug from a little girl that's two,
I picture in my head is soft as warm summer dew.
Summer dew is needed as it helps things to grow,
As little girls are needed to help daddies to know -
All there is to life is doing right by you,
I know there'll be mistakes, but let's just hope there
be few.
Remember that Daddy loves you with all his might,
And I'll ask God to watch over you every night.
Enjoy and have fun is all I can say,
I hope you have a very, very Happy Birthday.
God Bless you, Pumpkin.

Love always,
Daddy

Dear Dad:
From father to daughter and mother to son, they
just had to leave; their work must be done.
I think of that warm day in September; it was a
sad day, you have to remember.
I saw you standing so tall and so proud; you must
have felt good facing the crowd.
YOU told me, "be strong," but I just couldn't be. I
couldn't believe this had happened to me.
My father was leaving to go far away; I felt really
lonely what could I say?
As you were marching back to your truck, I blew
you a kiss and whispered, "good luck."
I watched as you drove by, all lonely and sad. I
just couldn't believe that it was my dad.
I SAID to myself, "Why take you?" Someone else
said, "He'll be back when he's through."
So now I am proud - proud of my dad. But don't
get me wrong - I often get sad.
I miss you so much, I guess you could say, as I
patiently wait for your homecoming day.
AS EACH day goes by, I often reminisce of when
I was small and you'd give me a kiss.
You write me some letters and I write you back,
but it's just not the same-it's your hugs that I lack.
And when you come home I can happily say, it
will be the best day of my life: Your homecoming
day.

Love, Jill.

4ª Bendición

Well I hope that when you recieve this letter you guys
are in the best of health. As for me I got sand all over. The
sandstorms are getting worst. The temp here is going higher
everyday. Yesterday it was 110°F. The climate here is
dry, thats way we don't feel it as much. But the sun
heats my bucket lunch everyday with in minutes. Dad, I
can't believe I am really here. I never knew what
these colors Red, white and blue really meant. Now I
know that these (colors don't run). My views on the
military have surely changed. I plan to reenlist and
maybe move up. But never leave the guard. I've had
a most excellent adventure when it comes to Saudi Arabia.
I knew the day I voloneetered I would never regret it.
And so far I haven't. Thanks to you and mom for letting
me choose my own path. And supporting me in everything
I do. I know I get crazy at times. But if it wasn't
for you urging me to make something out of the guard.
I would have never gone no where. Listen here I
send you a couple of pictures of me and stuff. Talk
to you next week. I love you. And remember
"These colors don't run"

love,

HI! Babygirl! How is everything back home? I miss you Alot, and my time is getting shorter, and shorter. But its not getting shorter quick enough for me or you. I received your packages one day after the other. THANKS baby. There is no doubt in my mine that I want to marry you. I guess now I realize how good of A wife you really could bee until now. Baby things here is not to good As you should already no. But I'm triing to do my best. Now I stay in my tent don't say to much to people. ME AND Chivers is still not speaking. Love you JASON. Burgess

The great state of New Jersey, like most states, had a handful of Pre-Mobilized Family Support Groups. The existing groups were 2-5 years old, strongly developed, and structured to conduct briefings on benefits and procedures on an everyday basis and during Annual Training. The groups also were involved in organizing the social activities of their units.

In August 1990, President Bush issued a "Presidential Callup" and Desert Shield began. As fate would have it, the units mobilized in New Jersey, did not have Pre-Mobilized Family Support Groups. Four members of the NJ Army and Air NCO Auxiliary, Dona Feldhann, Gale Goddard, Linda Fasulo, and Ann Zimmerman, came forward to assist in the development of the newly forming Support Groups.

All four of these volunteers were already Volunteer Battalion Level Family Support Coordinators. Diane Sodden, Mary Marshall, and Janet Douglass joined the volunteer list to help Mary Vey (253rd) and Ann Marie Cunningham (144th) develop their programs and support families in their respective areas.

Cpt. Robert (Budd) Springer, along with CWO (Ret.) Dan D'Amico and John Shepherd, Sr., were missioned as liasons to work with the mobilized troops and to oversee the assistance to the family members, as well as working with LTC Elizabeth Yull, State Family Program Coordinator.

Despite full time jobs, family responsibilities, and existing volunteer work, many volunteers (with and without loved ones in the Gulf), came forward to support MG Vito Morgano, the Adjutant General of N.J., promise to the soldiers to "make assistance

Ed Serrano is bid farewell by his son Elliot before leaving for Saudi Arabia.

Michael Panny with his "I love you" handsign that saw his daddy, SFC Ed Panny, off in September, now welcomes him home on May 28, 1991.

available on a 24 hour, 7 days a week basis, for their families."

Based on geographic location, four base support groups were set up to assist Desert Shield families, the Cape May Court House Armory (home of the 253rd), Hammonton Armory (home of the 144th), Sea Girt Military Academy (for Central Jersey families), and Jersey City Armory (for North Jersey). These groups soon became melting pots for all branches of the military, active, guard and reserve. Each of the 4 established a food pantry and a network of local services to assist the families during

emergency situations (i.e. auto and home repairs, medical and dental assistance, day care etc.).

The groups met once or twice a month to update the families and to handle problems. All those working in family support, full-time or volunteer, had late-night phone calls and missed family functions. In most cases spouses, if not activated, and children volunteered their time as well. There were always fast food dinners and days when nothing seemed right, but we kept on and each time someone said "thank you," it gave us the strength to give it

one more try to keep that promise made on a day that seemed so long ago.

It was noted from the beginning that the decrease in income experienced by the reserve component families would be the toughest thing to handle. The NCO Auxiliary started selling yellow ribbon bows with "because we care" printed on them at the Governor's review, September, 1990 and later sold patriotic wreaths. There were private individuals who created decorated door brooms and handmade sweatshirts.

Additional fundraisers developed within the support groups such as

On The Homefront

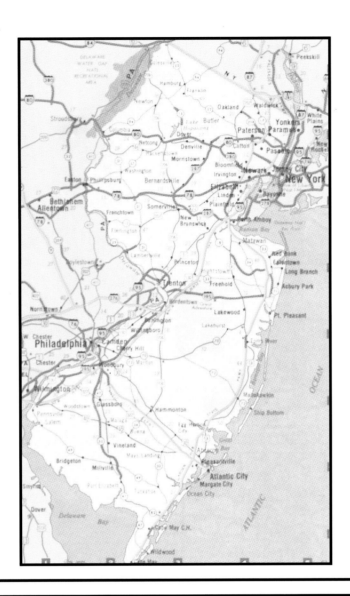

pancake breakfasts, beefsteak dinners, tee-shirt sales, Desert Shield/Storm pins etc. Donations came from private individuals and corporations. Companies and local organizations did food drives as well as gift certificate donations for local food chains.

The Vietnam Veterans of America, VFW, American Legion Posts, Red Cross Chapters, United Way, and County Departments, as well as the Community staffs of Fort Dix, McGuire AFB, Ft. Monmouth, Picatinny Arsenal, and the Coast Guard Station all networked with the support groups for assistance in all areas.

The support group coordinators, along with family members, formed the "Desert Shield/Storm Family Foundation, Inc." a non-profit organization registered in the state of New Jersey. The foundation is an all volunteer corporation and its Financial Aid Committee consists of Desert

Shield/Storm peers with careers ranging from housewife to banker. The foundation issues grants to Desert Storm families for emergency situations. The Executive Officers are: Cindy Ellis, President, Gale Goddard, Vice-President, Linda Fasulo, Secretary, and Ruth Burroughs, Treasurer.

The volunteer coordinators and family members attended inter-faith prayer services, the Governor's Super Bowl Party in the Meadowlands, a day on the boardwalk in Wildwood, shows in Atlantic City, a day at Great Adventure. They also testified during the open hearings of the State Assembly Military and Veterans Affairs Committee on "Problems Experienced by Desert Storm/Shield Families."

A special grant was issued and executed under Executive Order #29, to establish three state "Desert Storm Family Support Officers," under LTC William Lowe, Director, Division of

Veteran's Loans, Grants and Services. These three individuals made available the special services to all reserve component Desert Shield/Storm families and returnees on a full time basis. They will continue to do so for 180 days after the last N.J. unit returns home.

Governor Florio was the first to establish, under Executive Order #15, differential pay for state employees activated. Most counties and many municipalities followed suit.

It is impossible to list the over 800 individuals and corporate sponsors of the Desert Shield/Storm families. We "thank you" all from the bottom of our hearts.

Operation Oreo Cookie

Nabisco executives review sign for operation "Oreo Cookie."

Plane is readied to ship Oreo cookies overseas.

Brownie troop gets shipment of Girl Scout Cookies ready to ship to NJ National Guard Troops in Saudi Arabia.

Veteran' volunteer meets
Saudi veteran at
Philadelphia airport.

Welcome home signs lined
the G.S. Pkwy in
preparation for the 253rd's
homecoming.

LTC Joan Kakasick and CWO Roseanne Goodstein at farewell picnic.

The first stop for the troops upon arrival in the States.

State of New Jersey

DEPARTMENT OF MILITARY AND VETERANS' AFFAIRS

EGGERT CROSSING ROAD, CN 340
TRENTON, NEW JERSEY 08625-0340

JIM FLORIO
GOVERNOR
COMMANDER-IN-CHIEF

21 November 1990

VITO MORGANO
MAJOR GENERAL
THE ADJUTANT GENERAL

TO OUR NATIONAL GUARD FAMILY

Please let me take this opportunity to express my gratitude and offer my support to each and every spouse and loved one of all the magnificent members of our 144th Supply and Service Company.

Now more than ever the "Guard" appreciates your support.

Vito and I wish to offer our support to any of you who may need assistance. Please be aware that we have an active Family Support Program. The Unit Commanders and First Sergeants can obtain the names and agencies that are available for you. Lieutenant Colonel "Eliz" Yull (609-530-2815) and Captain Buddy Springer (609-561-0309) stand ready to provide the answers and offer solutions. Also, our wonderful Chaplains are always there for us in critical times around the clock.

This reinforces our firm belief that as a member of the New Jersey National Guard Family--you are never alone.

We all trust that these moments of uncertainty will pass; but, as usual, we are prepared to face the future.

God bless each and every one of you and I look forward to meeting you all in the coming year.

Sincerely,

Louise Morgano

A G.I. Family's Prayer

Hear, Lord, my prayer for my G.I.,
so eager to live — too young to die.

Beneath an alien blistering sun,
He faces a dangerous enemy gun.

The Storm clouds gather, the horror of war,
my soldier stands bravely guarding the door.

Defending justice, peace, and freedom,
to his Commander-in-Chief give Holy wisdom.

From wars' alarms, bring swift release.
Hasten the day of honorable peace.

On land and sand and sea and air,
I back my soldier with this prayer:

"No matter how far he's forced to roam,
just bring, I pray, my G.I. home."

AMEN

Robert H. Schuller
January 1991

*I support our G.I.'s
in the Persian Gulf!*

Ed and Betty Ann Sherretta of Cape May, are two of hundreds who celebrated Gulf cease-fire.

OPERATION DESERT SHIELD
Saudi Arabia

JANUARY 13, 1991
SUNDAY

DEAR CINDY:

Hi HONEY!! WELL I ARRIVED SAFE AND SOUND, GOT HERE AT 10:30 AM SATURDAY JAN 12,91. 2:30 AM YOUR TIME. SAUDI IS 8 HOURS AHEAD OF YOU. I AM WRITING YOU THIS LETTER BECAUSE RIGHT NOW IT IS A THREE HOUR WAIT FOR A TELEPHONE. I MAY TRY LATER, BUT FOR RIGHT NOW I HAVE TIME SO I DECIDED TO ~~RIGHT~~ WRITE. THE LIVING CONDITIONS ARE NOT TO BAD. WE ARE LIVING IN CONDO'S BELIEVE IT OR NOT. THE SAUDI GOVERNMENT BUILT THEM ABOUT 10 YEARS AGO FOR THE NOMADS, WHO NEVER OCCUPIED THEM. THEY ARE UNFURNISHED, BUT, AT LEAST THEY HAVE RUNNING WATER, INSIDE TOILETS AND IT IS A ROOF OVER OUR HEADS. HONEY, I DON'T KNOW IF YOU HAVE HEARD STORIES FROM THE OTHER WIVES SINCE THE UNIT GOT HERE, BUT MOST ARE NOT TRUE, IF NOT ALL ARE FALSE. WE HAVE NOT BEEN ATTACKED, THERE HAS BEEN NO TERRORIST ATTEMPTS, WE ARE ALL SAFE + WELL. I CAN NOT TELL YOU WHERE WE ARE OR WHERE WE WILL EVENTUALLY BE WORKING AT. ALL I CAN TELL YOU IS THAT WE ARE SAFE + WELL PROTECTED. WE ARE SEEMINGLY VERY IMPORTANT TO THIS OPERATION AND THEY ARE TAKING EVERY EFFORT TO PROTECT US.

OVER

© U.S. Allegiance Inc

YOUR LOVING HUSBAND

Joe

OX☐ OX☐ OX☐

Mary Vey at Interfaith Service.

Governor and Mrs. Florio and General and
Mrs. Morgano at the Interfaith Service.

Interfaith Service

...ening prayers at the Interfaith Prayer Service held on February 3, 1991.

Governor Florio gives message of hope at Interfaith Service.

Prayers are said by relatives of servicemen.

Interfaith Service held at Methodist Church, Cape May Court House.

Veteran and volunteers come together at homecoming.

The long wait is over for those who went and those who stayed "On the Homefront."

26 June 1991

Dear 144th. Family Support Group,

Just a few lines, saying hello, and to _thank_ you for your effort and perseverance in times that are as trying for you as well as us.

We are at Emerald City, our living quarters, and operating two separate Supply yards in our daily operation. The two companies that vacated the yards had over 100 personnel each, while we have roughly 20-25 people for each yard. Plus it is hot, 120°-126° more or less, but as long as we drink enough H_2O, we are allright.

I sincerely wanted you to know that of all the things you may have heard about the 144th there are two sides to every coin. And above all, God's Grace has sustained us, protected us, restrained many things that may work for evil, and it is that Grace, God's loving kindness and mercy that will bring us home. Sincerely, SGT. Patrick Spina.

Loving A Soldier
Is Not Always Gay

Loving a soldier is not always gay,
And loving him is a high price to pay.
It's mostly loving with nothing to hold,
It's being young, yet feeling old.

It's having him whisper his love to you;
It's whispering back that you love him too.
Then comes a kiss, a promise of love,
Knowing you're watched, approved from above.

Reluctantly, painfully, letting him go;
While you're dying inside from wanting him so.
Watching him leave with eyes full of tears.
Standing alone with hopes, dreams and fears.

It's sending a letter with the stamp upside down,
To a far away love in a far away town.
It's going to church to kneel and pray,
And really meaning the things that you say.

And though you know that he's far away,
You keep on loving him more each day.
Being in love will merit your dreams,
With thoughts of Heaven, where love's light gleams.

Days go by and no mail for a spell,
You wait for some word to hear that he's well.
Then the letter arrives and you're given to joy,
You're like a small child with a shining new toy.

With fingers a tremble and heart beating fast,
You tear open his letter and read it at last.
Yes, he is well, and misses you so;
And it's filled with the love you wanted to know.

Weeks are a month and months are a year;
You're awaiting the day you'll have no more fear.
Time passes slowly, yet it's gone very fast.
You're barely aware it is here till it's past.

Yes, loving a soldier brings bitterness and tears,
Loneliness, sadness and despondent years.
Loving a soldier really isn't much fun,
But it's well worth the price when the battle is won.

Remember, he's thinking of you every day.
He's sad and he's lonely for being away;
So love him, miss him, and try to be bolder,
And always be proud of loving a soldier.

Desert Shield

BCT staff photos/Dennis McDonald

Members of the 253rd Transportation Co., a National Guard unit from New Jersey, work out along the Persian Gulf.

Living on the edge of war

MOVE OUT

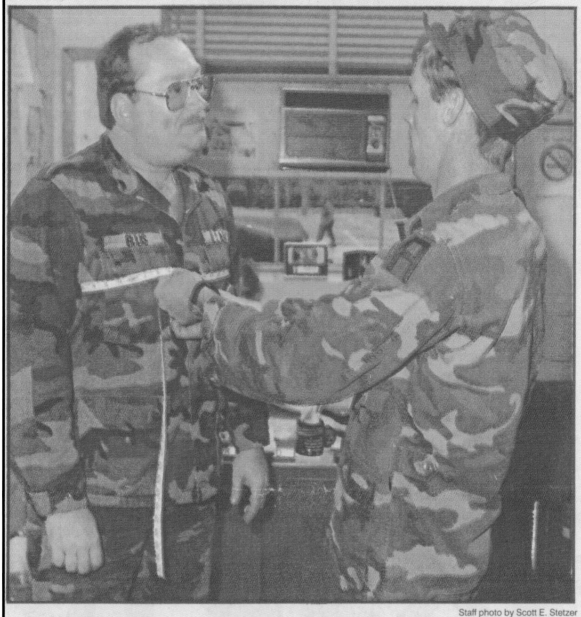

Staff photo by Scott E. Stetzer

Sfc. David Snyder measures Sgt. Joseph Ellis for new fatigues in Hammonton

'We've already postponed the honeymoon. If we have to, we'll go to a justice of the peace. But she would be disappointed.'

'My older son understands more than the others. He's really upset. He says, "Mom, what are you doing? Why don't you quit?" I tell them I've made a commitment.'

Preparations

Sand Camo is painted on new tanks to be deployed to Saudi Arabia at Military Ocean Terminal in Bayonne.

Welcome Home

Maldonado Family finally together again.

Lt Brown gets a welcome home hug.

THE ARMY WIVES SEAL

The eagle at the top of the circle represents the Army Wife, who in protecting her nest, also protects the flag and the future it represents. Alert and poised, she is ready to defend either when the need arises.

As the ultimate goal of her husband's profession is peace, so is it hers. The olive branch held by the eagle represents this peace; her hope for an end to wars for her husband and her children.

The lyre, symbol of harmony, gentility and romance, surrounds the four phases of her life that she holds dear.

The cradle represents her children, her Mother — her own Motherhood.

The sheaf of wheat represents the staples and stability she provides for her family — her duty.

The grapes represent the social life, the wine, fun, sense of humor — her lighter side.

The open book represents her individuality and personal self-fulfillment thru knowledge and wisdom. The person she is and becomes — her personal self.

The double circle enclosing all is her wedding band, symbol of eternity and never ending love. This circle is broken only by the eagle, here a symbol of her duty to country. For the Army Wife, the break in the circle represents the many separations and the possible ultimate sacrifice.

Ida True Terry — 1976

We Are The Guard's Family

It was our hands that let go, waving bravely as our father marched into the dark and thundering distance, marched courageously into the cannon's roar. ❧ <u>We are the Guard's family</u>, waiting patiently at the wooden gate for news of the battle -- the battle that rang freedom throughout this great land. ❧ We walk that battlefield in the mornings of our memories, we walk it in our own hearts, a place where death and sacrifice give way to creation; through our father's blood and our family's love was this great country born. ❧ <u>We are the Guard's family</u>.

❧

With open arms we await the return of our husbands, fathers, sons and brothers -- from Bunker Hill, Gettysburg and the world wars that threatened to end the world -- to end all that we love and understand and have fought for, the very heart of this great land. ❧ Patiently to this day we wait for their return from lands near and far: <u>we are the Guard's family</u>.

❧

We have watched, indeed imagined in our grief and dreams, our father's face change from loving companion and stalwart protector to the brave and anonymous countenance of the unknown Guard. ❧ It is he who brings love and comfort to sons and daughters of many languages, of many lands.

❧

Through our father's loving hands, we become the young son, comforted in the ravages of fire and war and flood; we become the mother reunited with her child, the daughter whose tears are finally dried. ❧ We watch as our father forges ahead in the starless dark against fear and sorrow, guardian of peace and freedom, protector of a better tomorrow. ❧ We, too, are protectors, keepers of freedom in our schools and communities. ❧ We would raise our own voices against those who oppose the unalienable right to live in equality and freedom-- to speak one's mind in the light and safety of day. ❧

❧

Our husbands and fathers, mothers and wives, sons and daughters return, <u>all Guards</u> from their missions of strife and peace; we rejoin hands, a family in the eternal march for freedom. ❧

KAREN LUSKY, daughter, ARNG

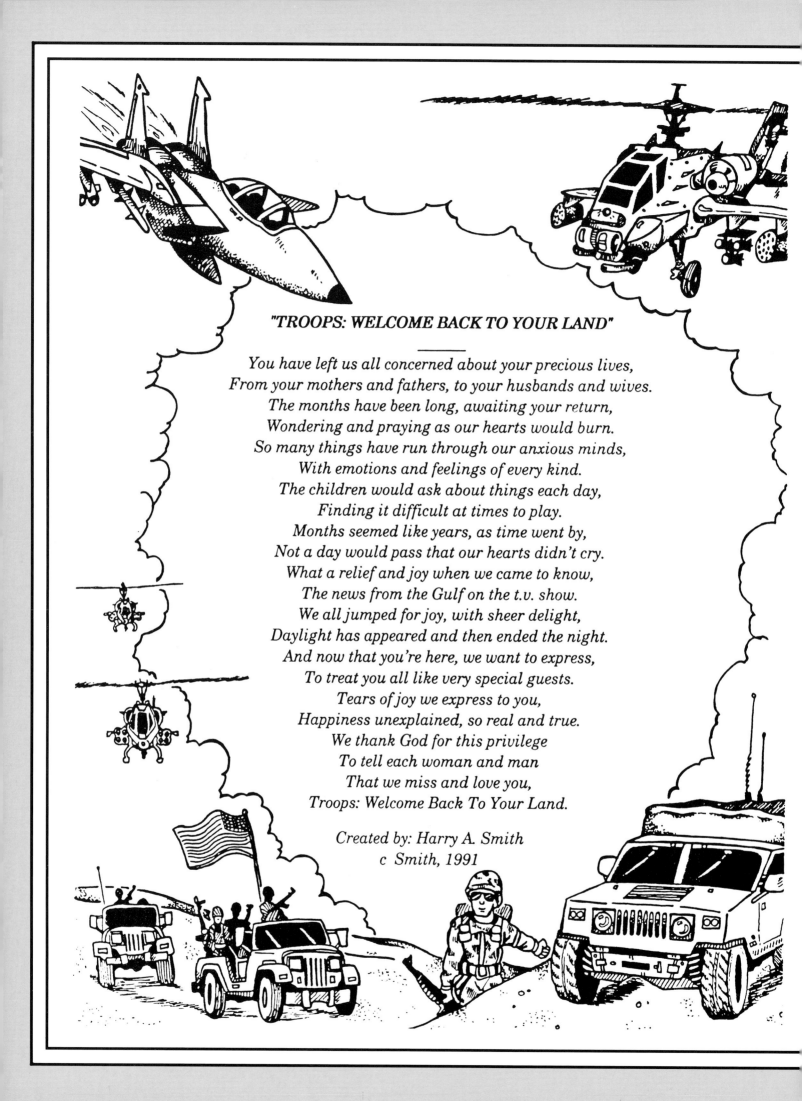

"TROOPS: WELCOME BACK TO YOUR LAND"

You have left us all concerned about your precious lives,
From your mothers and fathers, to your husbands and wives.
The months have been long, awaiting your return,
Wondering and praying as our hearts would burn.
So many things have run through our anxious minds,
With emotions and feelings of every kind.
The children would ask about things each day,
Finding it difficult at times to play.
Months seemed like years, as time went by,
Not a day would pass that our hearts didn't cry.
What a relief and joy when we came to know,
The news from the Gulf on the t.v. show.
We all jumped for joy, with sheer delight,
Daylight has appeared and then ended the night.
And now that you're here, we want to express,
To treat you all like very special guests.
Tears of joy we express to you,
Happiness unexplained, so real and true.
We thank God for this privilege
To tell each woman and man
That we miss and love you,
Troops: Welcome Back To Your Land.

Created by: Harry A. Smith
c Smith, 1991

5 Nov 91

Mr. D'Amico:

Thank you very much for all the help you have given me. I'm sorry for being such a pain to you. I also wish to thank you for the package you sent over the other day.

I'm very sorry for getting out of hand on the phone with you. I know you were trying to help me but I got very frustrated. I guess things are really starting to get to me. I know I'll feel better about everything when Fred comes home. Which I hope is very soon. So again I say thank you very much.

Sincerly
Joan

Family Support
Christmas Celebration

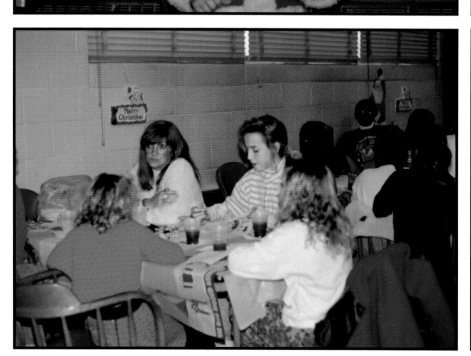

December 14, 1990
Cape May Court House

Left: Family Symposium held at High
Tech Center in November, 1990

Governor Florio, Brigadier General Taylor,
and Captain Springer review newly opened
food pantry in Hammonton.

328th Transportation Company's colors are
displayed as guidon fills in missing man
formation during pass & review,
Governor's Review, September, 1990.

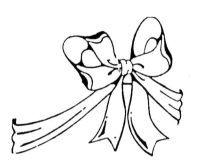

Letters from Enfield Elementary

Dear Mr. Panny,

When Mrs. Lockard told us that we were writing to you she started to cry. Well hi! My name is Chiara Lattanzio and I bet you can't pronounce it. I'm Italian because my mother is. I don't think you would get to this letter from all the other ones that you have to read. My brother is a pain in the neck. He beats me up every minute. Well back to me, I just got my report card and I did pretty well. I moved up to a higher group a month ago. My favorite show is the Simpsons and I love Art. You will find a picture that I made in the envelope. I'm ten years old and my birthday is in August 25th, 1980. I like ice skating. I am going skiing in February I can't wait.

From a person you don't know.
Chiara Lattanzio

Letters to Enfield Elementary

Dear Chiara,

Just a little note to let you know that it was very nice of you to write me and to let me know a little bit about yourself.

I hope that Christmas was okay for you and that you received the things that you wanted. My Christmas was okay, I worked the day and let my section take the day off.

I hope you like having my sister for a teacher. She is okay as sisters go, I guess. I am glad you got a good report card.

The weather over here is getting a little cooler now and the winds are starting to pick up. The wind makes the sand blow so hard that you cannot see where you are going.

Well it is time for me to run. I have more letters to write.
Your friend,
SFC E Panny

Above: Chiara Lattanzio, 4th grader from Enfield Elementary, with correspondence he had with SFC Ed Panny.

Cape May County
ARMY NATIONAL GUARD
Family Support Group

DESERT SHIELD

Pancake Breakfast

Date: November 11, 1990
Place: NATIONAL GUARD ARMORY
Parkway, CMCH
Time: 7AM - 12 noon

Adults $3.00 Donation
Children $2.00 Donation
Phones: 465-9610   465-5136

ric Panny serves orange juice to
heodore Farrell at Pancake Breakfast
eld at the NJNG Armory.

Speech Given By Michele Hawn At The Interfaith Service In Trenton 1/12/91

Dear Daddy,

It seems like only yesterday when you held me in your arms and told me you loved me. Tears rolled to my eyes and I fought to keep them back but you held me close and told me it was okay to cry.

I've tried so hard to understand why you must go away from me but I can't. You have your duties to our country I know, but this is so hard. You're so special to me I could never dream of losing you.

You're one of the most important people in my life and I love you so very much. I'm proud to have you for a father.

I cannot ever thank you enough for all that you have ever done for me. I'm behind you all the way and you never leave my thoughts or prayers. Daddy, I pray you come home soon for the pain of you being away hurts so much.

I miss you!! Love your Little Girl forever!!

Michele

Speech Given By Ruth Burroughs At The 253 Homecoming Ceremony

On September 30, 1990, the communities along with families, gave a send-off for the 253rd. A send-off that they would always remember. On that day, there were mixed emotions: pride that they were chosen because they were one of the best; sadness that they were taken away from their families; fear of the unknown, what was to lie ahead for them. On that day this unit bonded together and became a family, and, in turn, those of us they left behind become an extension of that family.

Today is our family reunion, and like proud parents that like to brag about their children, we are here to brag about ours. To say we are proud — so very proud — of your accomplishments, and your compassion for human rights and freedom.

WELCOME HOME SONS AND DAUGHTERS!!

The following was written and read by Arnette Splatt at the Cape May Court House Prayer Service.

The Prayer Of A Soldier's Mother

Dear God: Twenty five years ago, I prayed to you for a perfect baby, and you blessed me with the son I call Steven. And I prayed to you for guidance in raising him, and through you, I have a kind and loving Christian son. I prayed to you for the strength to endure his growing years, and when I faltered you held me up. And now God, he is thousands of miles from home, in a very, very hostile environment. I am praying to you for the courage for both of us to withstand these terrible days of war. I know you will bring him home to me, well and whole, for my faith, my love and my trust are in you, Lord.

Amen.

The following was composed and read by Ed Sherretta at the Trenton Prayer Service.

A Father's Prayer

My heart is in despair
My mind is in the air.

As each day goes by,
I find it easier to cry.

As a father you know
It's tough to see your son go.

For him I have a great deal in store
But one thing it's not, is war.

I know he's a man, I know he'll do good.
But, still I think, if I only could.

To watch his Mom suffer, is tough to do,
So I pray and pray he'll make it through.

Then, I realize it's not just my son,
But many a one.

God, please end this thing.
To the world, peace would you bring.

Wed 15 May 91 Gazette-Leader

Pen Pal serviceman comes home

By ART KEEGAN
Staff Writer

CAPE MAY COURT HOUSE -- When Joe Tedesco of the 253rd Transportation Company came home on emergency leave from the Middle East three weeks ago, he probably thought the hardest part was over.

He may have realized this assumption was untrue after meeting with his 20 pen pals from Middle Township Elementary School Number One last week.

The exuberant second graders welcomed their Persian Gulf pen pal with a "Welcome Home" T-shirt, greeting cards, a gold pin figure of America, cupcakes with a miniature American flag sticking out and a lollipop wrapped in yellow ribbon.

Aside from all the celebration, Tedesco, of Wildwood, tried to answer questions about the war the students might have had. Knowing the blunt honesty that many children present their thoughts with, this was by no means an easy task.

He held an informative discussion that would have tired Dick Cheyney replying to questions about chemical weapons, Saddam Hussein, the U.S. soldier's uniforms and participating in the surrender. It appeared some of the propaganda claiming the U.S. soldiers were aiming at Iraqi children caught the attention of these students because one student asked if the U.S. Air Force bombed children purposely.

"The only places the Allies and the United States Air Force bombed were isolations taken over by Suddam Hussein. Our job wasn't to hurt the civilians," explained Tedesco. "It was to get the military out (of Kuwait)."

Many students asked about the whole experience of being in a war.

"Our unit (the 253rd) was there for transporting the 82nd Airborne. We took the 82nd Airborne into Iraq."

Were you scared?

"I was thinking that I didn't want to get hit (by a bullet) and taken prisoner. I

Photo by Art Keegan

WELCOMED HOME by Middle Township Elementary School Number One second graders was Joe Tedesco of Wildwood. Before Tedesco, of the 253rd Transportation Company, came home on emergency leave he was a pen pal of Mrs. Henry's class.

was scared. It's a thing I'll never forget," replied Tedesco. "I hope none of you guys , when you get older, will have to go through it."

Tedesco, accompanied by his wife Cindy, said the support from Mrs. Henry's second grade class was inspirational. "From the beginning of the mobilization, I was getting cards and letters from these kids. It made me feel real real good," added Tedesco.

As a member of the 253rd, he was activated on Sept. 26 and departed from Cape May Court House to Fort Dix and ultimately left for Saudi Arabia on Nov. 7.

The students were ecstatic to get acquainted with their pen pal while assur-

ing his safe return to Cape May County. "We wanted him here because we wanted to make sure he was okay," said Jennifer Davies of Cape May Court House. "We also wanted to ask him questions about what he has doing over there."

"I think its fun to have him here because he was a soldier that was in real fighting so they (Kuwait) wouldn't lose the country," added Heather Garrison.

Although the students weren't directly involved with the. war, writing to someone gave them so type of realization about the horror of war. "They enjoyed writing letters," said Henry. "He wrote back and they were really excited about that. We hung up the letter. They were really anxious to meet him."

National Prayer Observance

*T*he men and women of the 170th Air Refueling Group gathered together on February 3, 1991 to observe a prayer for peace. In a very short, but moving ceremony, Chaplains William Sturges and Alphonse Stephenson offered scriptural passages in this ecumenical setting on the 170th flight line.

At the direction of President George Bush, we gathered, with all Americans, to rethink, rededicate and express our concern for the success of our joint efforts to liberate Kuwait and the well-being of all personnel in the Mideast area of responsibility.

Colonel James McIntosh addressed the gathered members in this solemn ceremony. He asked that we especially keep the activated members of the 170th in our prayers. The ceremony included scriptural readings by MSgt Edward Morton and SSgt Susan McIntyre of the 170th CAMS. ✈

THE WHITE HOUSE

November 26, 1990

Dear Mr. Goddard,

Thank you for your message and for letting
me know about your "Because We Care" project. I
am heartened by the number of Americans such as
you who are demonstrating their support for the
members of our Armed Forces.

This is a difficult assignment for our
service men and women, but efforts like yours,
that let them know that they have the backing
of the American people, surely make it a little
easier. Thank you for all you are doing in
behalf of those who are defending the cause
of freedom in the Persian Gulf.

The President joins me in sending our thanks
and best wishes.

Warmly,

Barbara Bush

Mr. Gale Goddard
Apartment 58
1420 18th Avenue
Wall, New Jersey 07719

1-3-91

Please accept my heart felt "Thank you" to those who have tried to help with our personal problems these past months.

Also thanks for the gift certificates S K Mart & Shop rite. They certainly were of help. Jason chose to buy a sweater with his gift money.

Once again, many thanks to you all for the work you are doing here. We continue to pray for the safe return of all members of the 253rd, and all members of our armed forces.

Sincerely
Beverly Gurdgiel & family

Top: Col. Pierce and Gale Goddard thanking volunteers. Above: Teacher Donna Koch and her students of Memorial Middle School, Bricktown, with check to be presented to Gale Goddard and Central Family Support.

Gulf troops' kids need help coping

By LAURA ITALIANO
Staff Writer

Mary Vey understands why, for a month now, her 9-year-old daughter Christine hasn't taken off the small gold cross the little girl wears around her neck.

"She tells me she won't take it off, 'Dad gave it to me,' " says Vey, a North Wildwood mother of four, and one of the nearly 100 parents left behind with the children while their spouses are stationed in the Persian Gulf as part of the Army National Guard 253rd Transportation Company, which is based in the Cape May Court House Armory.

When daddy or mommy go off to war, children may throw temper tantrums, feel guilty or depressed, and even cling, like little Christine, to a favorite memento.

The parents who stay behind need to be understanding of their children's feelings as the whole family learns to cope with the separation, say experts within the military and the growing field of parent child separation.

A noted Harvard psychiatrist, an Army consultant, a parent educator and a local family systems therapist each have similar things to say about what happens to the children when a parent trades home base for a military base.

What follows are the warnings and advice of these experts — Mary Vey included.

Mary Vey, mother of four and wife of Sgt. Michael Vey, platoon sergeant with the 253rd Transportation Company:

Mary Vey's husband. Michael, was in a military school in Arkansas when the Vey family got the news: Michael would be coming home on Sept. 22, and would leave the following week for Ft. Dix. From Ft. Dix, there was every likelihood Michael and his company would head straight for the Persian Gulf.

"It's funny, but we were more upset when he was in Ft. Dix, because it was all so new," Mary Vey said in a recent interview. By the time Michael arrived in the Persian Gulf, on Nov. 9th, the Vey family had begun to learn to cope.

Guardsman Returns To Students' Awe

By AL CAMPBELL

WILDWOOD — Desert dust on his boots was all Spec. Dave Moyer had to show Glenwood Avenue Elementary School pupils of his Desert Storm service with the 253rd Transportation Co.

Still, the soldier was a star in their eyes Wednesday. He joined Warrant Officer Dan D'Amico, Mary Vey and Marge Panny, all representing the National Guard unit's Family Support Group, to accept a student-raised $400 gift for unit families.

STUDENTS' from the Special Education classes made yellow ribbons, and sold them. That brought in $350. Others served breakfast to teachers recently in the school's Blue Chip Cafe, and raised an additional $50 in tips, to help raise the total.

Moyer, a union carpenter from Green Creek, returned from the Persian Gulf region March 1 following a Feb. 14 truck accident on Dodge Highway which resulted in his being given medical leave and early return from the war zone.

"Somebody cut me off. I was driving a five-ton cargo truck, one of the new ones, and I rolled it over," Moyer said.

"THAT (highway) is going to be famous someday," he added. "That's the one where they moved all the equipment and a 60-day supply of food and fuel toward the west" for the ground offensive against Iraqi forces.

Some students gazed up at him, others touching his camouflage uniform, while still others fired machine-gun like questions.

Others looked at items brought by Panny that were sent home by her husband, Sgt. James Panny, also of Green Creek. Among them were American cereal boxes in traditional colors and names, but with Arabic

Al Campbell

HERE'S YOUR HAT — Jason Casher, 7, of Wildwood returns Spec. Dave Moyer's camouflage hat Wednesday at the end of a visit when $400, raised by students, was presented to the 253rd Transportation Company's Family Support Group. Jason's the son of Patricia Huach.

writing elsewhere.

What did it mean? they puzzled. Moyer couldn't answer them.

"WE WANT you all to know we really appreciated all your yellow ribbons and everything else you did to remember us while we were over in the desert," Moyer said.

"First, we were at the port waiting for our trucks to arrive," Moyer said.

"Then, we were attached to the 82nd Airborne, he added, glancing down to the black and green patch sewn on his uniform's left breast pocket.

"Once we were attached there, we were moved into the desert to a placed call Rafha," he said.

"EVERYBODY was fine and they're all looking forward to getting home," the solider said.

After 30 days' medical leave, he'll report to Bethesda Naval Hospital for evaluation. Then, it's possible he'll be released for treatments at the Coast Guard base or some other military installation.

He resides in Green Creek with his wife, Chris, and 19-month old son.

Girl Ponders War's Meaning

NORTH WILDWOOD — Jolene Stevenson, a Seventh grader at Margaret Mace Elementary School here, has written a poem expressing her feelings about the war in the Persian Gulf. Says Jolene:

Desert Storm
Saddam Hussein said he would reign,
He stole Kuwait and felt no shame.
To me the fighting is very sad.
But it must be done, for Hussein is mad.

U.S. Patriots hit the Scuds,
But they still fall on Israel with a thud.
We should reach out and give a hand,
To all the troops in the desert sand.

I am glad our president does all he can do.
To give support, which you should give too.

Willum O'Connell

PEACEFUL SUPPORT — April Garrison, 8, Alberta Garrison, and Billie Jo Garrison, 9, all of Wildwood show support for the 253rd Transportation Company during Saturday's "South Jersey Joins Hands" rally in Rio Grande. Although a four-mile human chain didn't materialize to link Lower and Middle townships, spirits were upbeat as a ceasefire in the Persian Gulf seemed likely. April and Billie Jo are children of Mr. and Mrs. William Garrison.

Troop Support Set For Easter

WILDWOOD — An appreciation day for our troops' efforts in the Persian Gulf war will be held here on the boardwalk Easter Sunday, March 31.

Two miles of yellow ribbon will deck the promenade, and everyone who attends is asked to bring flags. Veterans are encouraged to come in uniform.

Names of service people with the 253rd Transportation Division will be written on the ribbon. Anyone with a relative serving in a group other than the 253rd is encouraged to call Barbara Waterman at 522-2466, so that their name may also be inscribed.

Celebrate Troop Homecoming

WILDWOOD — A salute to local service people will take place Easter Sunday at the bandshell at Schellenger Avenue and the Boardwalk at 1 p.m.

A two-mile yellow ribbon will deck the Boardwalk, inscribed with names of the troops. All veterans are asked to join the observance in uniform. Call 522-4646 or 522-2466 for more information.

253RD'S ADDRESS

The following is a new mailing address, announced March 7, for members of the 253rd Transportation Company serving in Saudi Arabia:

Name/Rank/Soc. Sec. No.
253rd Trans Co.
68th Trans Bn
APO New York, 09899

ENDS TRAINING

CAPE MAY — Navy Seaman Recruit Michelle D. Hayes, daughter of Linda S. Hayes of 81 Atlantic Ave., has completed recruit training at Recruit Training Command, Orlando, Fla.

Thanks for support

To the Editor:

The Greater Cape May Chamber of Commerce wishes to thank everyone for their support of the Christmas production "Once Upon A Time on a Victorian Christmas Eve" held at Cape May Convention Hall, Sunday, Dec. 16.

The "Volunteer Production Company" did an outstanding job of providing an evening of entertainment for one and all. Four thousand and five hundred dollars were raised to provide Christmas dinners for military families with members serving overseas in "Operation Desert Shield," some needy area families, and service organizations. Food certificates will be purchased and Shop Rite Food Stores, in support of this project, gave additional certificates and coupons.

With the genius and dedication of Ricky Deodati (executive and musical director) and the boundless creativity and enthusiasm of Victoria Biederman (artistic director), we all experienced an evening filled with the true meaning of the holiday season.

So many people gave time, materials, talent, and money. Everything (and we do mean everything) was donated by you - the people of this community. To list all of you would fill this newspaper.

This holiday season is a trying one - emotionally and economically. This benefit production proves hands-down that our community cares - gives - and can pull together to attain a common goal. We needed this more than ever this year and we got it!

Thank you all very much.

For Terry Brown and the Cape May Recreation Department -- you were great!

Shirley Goodroe
Board of Director
Chamber of Commerce
of Greater Cape May

The following was written and read by Angie Longo, at the Cape May Court House Prayer Service.

My name is Angie Longo. My father is Staff Sergeant Stanley Longo. I guess I could begin by telling you about the emotions I've been feeling.

Scared: **This is at the top of my list. Scared something might happen to my Dad.**

Helpless: **Helpless when I see my Mother cry and all I can do is give her a hug.**

Thankful: **Thankful I have a lot of supportive friends and family.**

Strong: **Strong in my belief that things will be back to normal.**

Glad: **Glad that I live in a country where I can express myself outloud.**

Angry: **Angry that people are protesting on our streets. They don't realize the danger they are doing to morale. They couldn't possibly have a loved one over there.**

Proud: **Most of all Proud, that my father went when his country said they needed him.**

Last but not least
Hopeful: **Hopeful they will all be home safely soon.**

> 'I saw children with none of the things we have. Their parents are shepherds and tend the sheep and goats. The children had no school to go to. We are very blessed.'
> Staff Sgt. Ronald Kent

Press photos by Joyce Vanaman

Staff Sgt. Ronald Kent of the 253rd National Guard unit, with son Joshua on his lap, talks to class about his duty in Gulf War

School 'hero'
Millville soldier visits son's class

By JOYCE VANAMAN
Staff Writer

MILLVILLE — Bursting with pride as his dad answered questions of his kindergarten classmates Friday, Joshua Kent, 5, stuck very close to Staff Sgt. Ronald Kent of the Army National Guard Transportation 253rd Unit out of Cape May Court House.

A real "hero" to the youngsters in Sharon Riley's kindergarten class, Kent, 36, brought with him samples of a typical meal he had in the Persian Gulf, such as dried beef with gravy, crackers and dehydrated fruit.

They couldn't match the pork chops, cabbage and hot rolls his wife, Annette, cooked for him Thursday night.

Before Kent went into Joshua's classroom, he participated in an outdoor flagraising ceremony. Standing on the school steps, he watched, along with some 350 elementary pupils and teachers as his wife, son and daughter Tiffany, 12, a seventh-grader at Holly Heights School, raised the flag. He helped lead the flag salute.

Kent received a Presidential Fitness Badge from Ralph "Rocky" Musarra, physical education teacher and adviser of the Student Leaders, which sponsored the flagraising project.

Principal Roger Simpkins explained that in February Kent's family had participated in a similar flagraising ceremony. That ceremony honored Kent, the only parent of a current Bacon

Kent, with son Joshua, 5, wears desert-camouflage uniform

School student to serve in the Persian Gulf, and two others.

Nick Nixon, son of head custodian Keith Nixon, and John Miller, a former Bacon student, also were honored. Nixon served aboard the USS Kennedy, while Miller served aboard the USS Portland. A videotape of that ceremony was sent to Kent, Simpkins said.

Kent, who arrived home April 5 on convalescent leave, thanked the students and staff for their support. "As of last night (Thursday), the war officially was over, but there are still Americans there. I ask for your continued support," said Kent.

Then he went to Joshua's class, where a "Welcome Home" banner was hung. Giving him a hug and in-

troducing Kent to the class, Riley told the students, "We're very lucky to live in America."

And Kent agreed, telling the youngsters, "I saw children with none of the things we have. Their parents are shepherds and tend the sheep and goats. The children had no school to go to. We are very blessed."

"How bad was the war?" asked a youngster. "Whenever anyone has to die, it's bad, but it had to be done," Kent replied.

"Are you glad to be here?" asked Thomas Perugini. "I am very glad to be out of the war," Kent said.

"What are those things on your chest?" asked Nashea Thomas, 5. Kent's uniform bore tan and brown desert-camouflage colors.

"How do you feel?" asked another student. "Often I felt tired because we didn't get much sleep. My company was a truck company and sometimes we drove 700 to 800 miles," Kent said.

Kent told The Press that his unit was attached to the 82nd Airborne Infantry, which took 77 enemy prisoners of war on "G Day," the first day of the gound war.

Annette Kent said she drove her husband home last Friday from Walter Reed Army Medical Center in Washington, D.C. He will be returning there Monday for more tests.

"I had back surgery there in 1988, and I reinjured my back in Iraq bouncing around on the trucks," Sgt. Kent said.

Singers and Musicians...

FIRE TRUCK DISPLAYS...

A VISIT FROM
THE EASTER BUNNY!...

MUSICAL

Arts and Crafts!...

TRIBUTE

FREE EVENT!
OPEN TO THE
PUBLIC!

EASTER EGG
HUNT
FOR THE KIDS!...

TO OUR

Bake Sale...

Contests...

TROOPS!

CLOWNS...

fun for everyone!!!

Saturday, March 23, 1991

1 p.m. to 3 p.m.

(Rain Dat
March 2

Location : Fairgrounds of
Gloucester County College
Tanyard Road, Deptford

Sponsored by
The Persian Gulf Support Group
at Kennedy Memorial Hospitals -
Washington Township Division

VOLLEY ROUND THE TROOPS

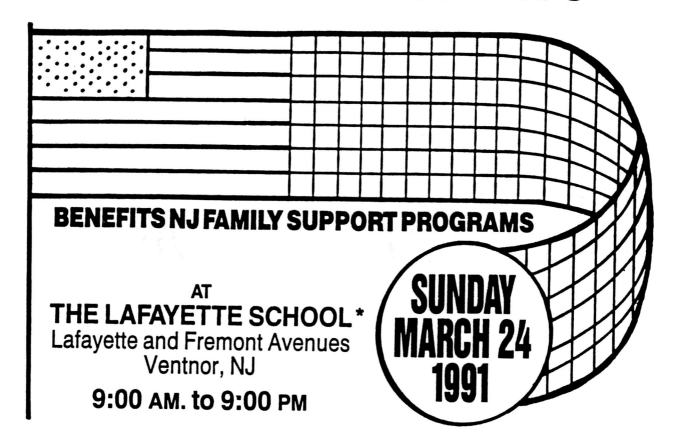

BENEFITS NJ FAMILY SUPPORT PROGRAMS

SUNDAY MARCH 24 1991

AT
THE LAFAYETTE SCHOOL*
Lafayette and Fremont Avenues
Ventnor, NJ

9:00 AM. to 9:00 PM

DONATIONS: $10⁰⁰ PER PERSON/PER HOUR
MINIMUM 6 PLAYERS PER HOUR

FOR MORE INFORMATION CALL
Maloney's
(609) 823-3546

AFTER THE GAME, FREE BUFFET AT
Maloney's
23 S. WASHINGTON AVENUE
MARGATE, NJ
12:00 Noon till ?

*PENDING BOARD APPROVAL

Rio Grande Plaza
"Cape May County Proud"

Four Days of Entertainment & Fun, May 30 to June 2

FLAG RAISING CEREMONY

9:30 a.m., Thursday, May 30

Music
By the Lower Cape May Regional
High School Band

Honor Guard
From The 154th NJ National Guard

Puppet Shows

"Great American Teddy Bears"
by the Brownstone Puppet Theater
10:30 a.m., noon, 1:30 p.m. & 4:30 p.m.
Thurdsay, May 30 & Friday, May 31
Handshaking appearance by Annabelle Bear

"Ben & Me"
A fun look at Ben Franklin by the
Tom Lohrman Puppeteers
10:30 a.m., noon, 1:30 p.m. & 4:30 p.m.
Saturday, June 1
12:30 p.m. and 2:30 p.m. Sunday, June 2

Music

"Cape May County String Band"

7 p.m. Thursday, May 30
7 p.m. Friday, May 31
1 p.m. Sunday, June 2

"Four For The Road"
Barbershop style strolling and singing
2 p.m. - 4 p.m. Thursday, May 30
Friday, May 31, Sunday, June 2

"Summer Sounds"
Dixieland Music
7:30 p.m. Saturday, June 1

"Ribbon of Support for Our Military"

2 p.m. - 4 p.m., Saturday, June 1

Put a dollar—or more—on a ribbon that stretches from end to end of the shopping center.
All donations benefit returning Persian Gulf military personnel and their families through the 253rd & 144th NJ National Guard
Family Support Groups. Radio time will be donated by WBNJ. Area Scouts will be on hand. We hope that you will be, too!

FROM THE MIDDLE EAST

The Basic Skills department sent a holiday banner to Sgt. Maston, son of our secretary, Mrs. Maston. They received a thank you note from him. We share it with all of you.

To the Children and Staff
Basic Skills Depart,

Thank-you so much for the holiday banner! It brought smiles to the faces of all of us. It certainly is nice to receive things such as these from home. Your support is important to us

I hope your holidays were good ones

Thanks again and please take care

Sincerly,
Sgt R.S Maston

Sempa Fidelis!

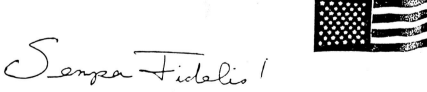

President B____
The White H____
1600 Penna. ____
Washington, ____

Dear Mr. Pr____

My N____
Today I fe____
have the fr____
ried about ____
we finish; ____

The Little Warrior

Glenwood Ave. School
Wildwood, N.J.

DEAR MR. PRESIDENT:

Sixth grade students
at Elementary #1
wrote letters to
President Bush to
express their
concerns , feelings,
and thoughts . Here
is a sample from
Tyquine Wilson of
6A.

Glenwood Ave. School
Wildwood, N.J. 08260
January 17 1991

nt:

is Tyquine Wilson and I am eleven years old.
d because my uncle is in Saudi Arabia. I think we
o fight because Saddam can't take over Kuwait. I am wor-
fighting because he might get killed. My wish is that
war peacefully Please let there be peace!

Sincerely yours,
Tyquine
Wilson

CONCERNED

As we look around Glenwood Avenue School and listen in the classrooms, we become very aware that children and teachers are very concerned about the Middle East and its problems. We can see that our hearts are going out to the soldiers. Everywhere we can see yellow ribbons - on the walls, on peoples' shirts, on the windows, in the classrooms and on doors. Some students are writing in their journals about the war. We hear news reports. Some boys and girls are writing letters, making banners, and even making videos.

In this newspaper you will read about the many concerns of our students about the war, the soldiers, and their families, and peace.

We dedicate this issue of our newspaper to peace.

The Special Education Department students under the guidance of Ms. Fran Finocchiaro, Ms. Nancy Barton, and Miss Judy Tague, at Glenwood Avenue School can be seen working very hard making yellow ribbons trimmed with red, white, and blue in honor of the 253rd Transportation Company that is now in Saudi Arabia. The 253rd Division has Cape May Court House as its homebase and many of our students have family members in this troop. The students all had jobs in this project. Some children were cutting the ribbons in different sizes. Other boys and girls were tying the red, white and blue ribbons together. Some of the students sell these ribbons daily throughout the school. Posters were created and hung throughout the schools to advertise this project. Ms Fin told us, "It was wonderful seeing all the children getting along and working very hard to finish this project. The children were so happy to see everyone buying their ribbons and wearing them. The children count their profits daily and this has brought them new experiences with money and a great sense of pride." Anyone can purchase these ribbons in Ms. Fin's room, Room 225, and in Mrs. Mitchell's Elementary #1 classroom, Room 214. The cost of this beautiful ribbon is $1.00. The profits from this project will be donated to the families of the 253rd Company. We care about these men and women who are fighting for our country and hope they come home safely soon.

written by:
The Special Education Department

On Th

Here is a sample of the work outside Mrs. Carroll's second grade classroom entitled "Our Hearts Are With You".

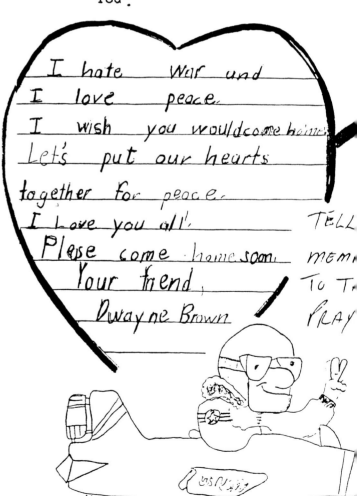

I hate War und
I love peace.
I wish you wouldcome home
Let's put our hearts
together for peace.
I Love you all.
Plese come home soon.
Your friend,
Dwayne Brown

TELL
MEM
TO T
PRAY

Homefront

The fifth and sixth graders also sent letters to the Middle East in care of Karen and Kelly Nickerson's father. Here is a portion of the letter returned to Glenwood Avenue School from their father who is in the 253rd Trans. Co.

...RY ONE FOR MYSELF AND THE

OF THE 253RD TRANS. CO WISH

YOU FOR YOUR THOUGHTS AND

SINCERELY
SPC. LAWRENCE MURDOCK

Gr.5

TO: Soldiers of the Big "253"

...I'M WITH YOU ALL THE WAY!

Just thought I'd write to let you all know that you're not forgotten. As a fellow Guardmember I know what it means to be a citizen soldier and the personal sacrifices you endure. Rest assured that your contributions are appreciated by all Americans, especially us in the NJNG (Army & Air). We are proud of you and eagerly await your return. My prayers are with you all. God speed for a safe and quick return.

Sincerely,
Ron & Maryann Cefalone
(COMPTROLLER, USPFO-NJ)

P.S.
Don't forget to do your "PMCS", ya got a good shot at winning the Maint Excellence award for FY 91 (HA! HA!) I thought you guys could use some humor! ☺

Vineland high school class backs U.S. troops with sale of T-shirts

By DIANE D'AMICO
Staff Writer

VINELAND — Students in the 10th grade marketing class at Vineland High School North are learning about sales by showing their support for the troops in the Persian Gulf.

The students involved in DE-CA (Distributive Education Classes of America) are selling specially made blue T-shirts decorated with a yellow ribbon and the words that the shirt is worn in honor of all U.S. military personnel in the Middle East in hope for their safe return. Those with a friend or family member in the gulf can have that person's name monogrammed on the shirt for an additional fee.

The shirts are this year's civic consciousness project coordinated with teacher Wilbert Cooper. Last year the students had a Drug Free-That's Me promotion.

Cooper, an Air Force veteran, worked up the T-shirt design. Proceeds from the sales will pay for the students' DECA dues and expenses to go the Southern Regional DECA Conference.

"The project gives the students exposure to civic activities in the community," Cooper said. "And it also gives them a chance to put their classroom work into action."

About 190 shirts have been sold so far at $8 each, or $12 with monogramming. They can be ordered by calling Cooper at the school at 794-6815.

"The shirts are pretty easy to sell because a lot of people want to show their support for the troops," student Madelyn Rosario said.

Olga Quinones said her mother wants one because her cousin is in the gulf, and the local Desert Shield support group is also interested in buying the shirts.

Cooper has also sold quite a few because he lives near Dover Air Force Base in Delaware.

"People see them and order them for others, too," he said. "We've sent some to Maryland."

While the project is a sucess, the students are concerned that their entire course may be eliminated. The program is supposed to run for three years, but this year it is only being offered in the 10th grade.

Press photo by Dale

Dawn Nelson displays a T-shirt sold by marketing class

Vineland Developmental Center
Employees' Association

1676 East Landis Avenue
Vineland, New Jersey, 08360

DESERT STORM

Operation Desert Storm has caused the call-up of many of our area's reservists. This has left their families with only their military pay to feed and house the spouses and children left home. These families are in bad need of non-perishable foods, can goods, and in many cases diapers. The VDCEA is sponsoring a drive to assist these families. Bring in a can of food, box of cereal, or diapers and drop off at the following locations;

West Campus
TLC-Recreation

East Campus
MPB-Recreation
Canteen
Switchboard
Hospital Lobby

If your cottage or work area has too much to bring to one of these locations, call Vito, 6086, to arrange pick-up.

They Returned To Teach The Children

SFC Ed Panny explains moves the troops made through Saudi Arabia into Iraq to the students of the Enfield Elementary School.

Visiting Hearing Impaired Class at the Ocean Academy School, Cape May Court House.

R And R
In The Gulf

Aboard The Cunard Princess

Please Join Us for A

"SALUTE TO THE TROOPS"

to Benefit Desert Storm Support Groups of New Jersey

Date: July 4th, 1991

Time: 10 AM to 10 PM

Place: Lake Lenape Park
Park Road & 13th Street
Mays Landing, New Jersey
625-2021

Admission: $5.00 per person

......GREAT FUN FOR THE ENTIRE FAMILY.......

- Amusements - Live Entertainment - Spectacular Fire Works Display -
- Swimming - Picnicking - Great Food* - Boating* - Water Sports* -
-TV 40 & WMGM Celebrity Softball & Volleyball Tournaments-

Sponsored by: Lake Lenape Park   *Extra Charge
TV 40 - WMGM Radio

HELP MAKE THIS BENEFIT ONE OF THE LARGEST EVER!

SEE YOU ON THE 4TH!

Send a message to someone you love stationed in the Gulf. For free.

Desert Fax℠ service can help you reach U.S. Military Personnel in the Gulf.*

A quick note. A silly doodle. A clipping from the local newspaper. They may not seem like much, but to someone far away from home, they can mean a lot. And now there's a fast, easy way to send these heartfelt messages to a loved one stationed in the Gulf. For free.

It's called Desert Fax. It stores messages electronically and transmits them at high speed using Enhanced FAX service, which is available internationally. So you can fax a message to any U.S. military personnel overseas** involved in Operation Desert Shield.

Just cut out the Desert Fax form along the dotted line on the opposite page and put your personal message in the space provided.† Then make a photocopy of the form and bring it, complete with the necessary information including social security number and APO/FPO, to your nearest AT&T Phone Center. An employee will fax it for you. And the person in the Gulf should receive your message within a few days.

Desert Fax messages can only be sent from the U.S. to the Gulf using the official form shown here, or forms available at all AT&T Phone Centers. To find out where the one nearest to you is located, and its hours, consult your white pages. Or call 1 800 555-8111, Ext. 36, Mon-Fri 8am-6pm, Sat 8am-4pm.

Because staying connected is something that's important to all of us.

Desert Fax is a public service brought to you by AT&T.
This space is donated by this publication.

When you call, give operator your zip code and they will tell you the closest ATT Phone Center.

*This service will remain in effect until modified or withdrawn by AT&T
**Active Duty and Reservists   †Blue or black ballpoint pen recommended

Middle Township signature board.　Sgt. Charles Unangst Family at Family Day Picnic, October, 1990.

Delores Santese and Mary Anne Imler, civilian volunteers, sew patches on uniforms.

Carol Fols and Lorraine Fowler Springer, civilian volunteers, sew patches on uniforms.

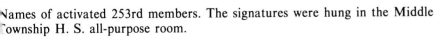
Names of activated 253rd members. The signatures were hung in the Middle Township H. S. all-purpose room.

Mrs. Morgano and Rose Scott at the Family Picnic.

"SUPPORT THE STORM"
MUSIC FESTIVAL
AT
CAPE MAY CONVENTION HALL
SUNDAY MARCH 10th 1991
6:00 to 10:00 PM
TO BENEFIT THE FAMILY SUPPORT GROUP OF THE 253rd
TRANSPORTATION UNIT IN OPERATION DESERT STORM
LOCAL BANDS TO APPEAR
HIGH TENSION
TWELVE:01
SLAM JAZZ
POSSE
A FESTIVAL OF MANY SOUNDS AN ARRAY OF MUSIC
SOMETHING FOR EVERY ONE
ORIGINALS TOP 40 SOUTHERN ROCK JAZZ AND NEW
WORLD
TICKETS $5.00 $7.00 DAY OF SHOW
TICKETS ON SALE AT MR. J'S MUSIC KROWN RECORDS NOTE
FOR NOTE MUSIC VIBRATION'S MUSIC, AND BAYSHORE
VARIETY FOR MORE INFO. CALL 886-7282
OR 884-2027

Cape May County
ARMY NATIONAL GUARD
Family Support Group

DESERT SHIELD

Pancake Breakfast ☕
and Bake Sale

Date: November 11, 1990
Place: NATIONAL GUARD ARMORY
Parkway, CMCH
Time: 7AM - 12 noon

Adults $3.00 Donation
Children $2.00 Donation
Phones: 465-9610   465-5136

TICKETS AVAILABLE AT ARMORY
OR FROM NATIONAL GUARD MEMBERS.

New Year's Eve

1SG William Cloer.

Sgt. Carmen Santiago and SFC David Pearson.

144th New Year's Party at Fort Dix.

LT. Leslie T. Carter.

PT. James Casalunova

SPC. Joe Vandervort

SFC Arturo Ramirez and SGT. Santiago Rivera

Fort Dix

Everybody loves a parade!

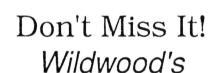

Happy Easter!

Don't Miss It!
Wildwood's
APPRECIATION DAY
for the
U.S. ARMED FORCES
Easter Sunday
March 31, 1991
1:00 P.M. on the Boardwalk
2 Mile Yellow Ribbon!

98.7 FM

WLQE

lucky **99** COUNTRY

Presents...

OPERATION HOMEFRONT

A Benefit for families of 253rd Nat'l Guard Unit

SUNDAY NOV. 4 , 7PM

LIGHTHOUSE POINTE

5101 Shawcrest, Wildwood

LIVE COUNTRY MUSIC

With:

Country Joe Liptok

Southbound

Ray Ballou

Johnny Tacco & Keith Hickman

And

Midnight Fire

MUSIC, FOOD, PRIZES

DONATION: $5.00

253rd families preparing float for parade.

253rd children's Christmas party sponsored by the Family Group at the Cape May Court House Armory.

Governor's Super Bowl Party '91 at the Meadowlands. Governor Florio, Jennifer Gautier and Arika Hemphill.

Easter celebrations of the 144th families.

The day the 144th left for Fort Dix.

$4,000 check is displayed by the Monroe
Township H. S. cheerleaders who helped raise
the money.

WANTS YOU TO ATTEND THE

"MASH BASH"
BENEFIT

ON SATURDAY, DECEMBER 15TH
AT 2100 HOURS

To Benefit The Families Of The
253RD TRANSPORTATION COMPANY

Don't Miss This Outrageous Party
$1.25 Drinks Till 11:00

Klinger Look-Alike Contest
Free "RADAR" Detector Giveaway
Prizes for the Best Military Apparel
We will be making a video
at Cheers to cheer up the troops overseas!

Please support the 253rd Transportation
Company Benefit!

3400 Pacific Ave.
Wildwood, New Jersey
729-3900   522-2048

Spaghetti Dinner
All "U" Can Eat
Friday, March 8, 1991
5 to 8 p.m.
at Marmora Firehouse

Benefits 253rd Trans. Co.
Family Support Group

$5.00
Adult

$3.00
Children

Sponsored by

All Upper Township Fire Companys
and Rescue Squad

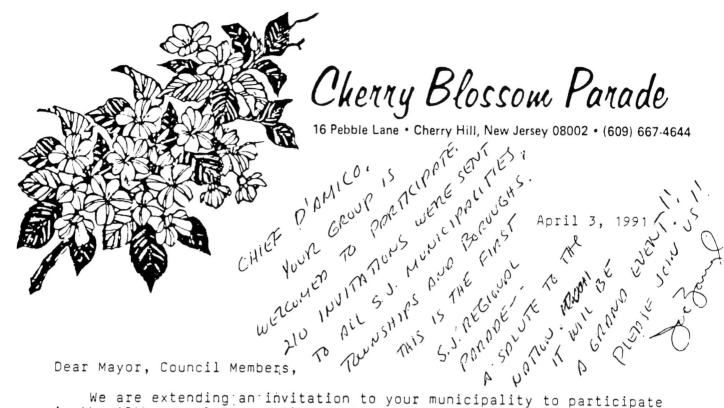

Cherry Blossom Parade

16 Pebble Lane • Cherry Hill, New Jersey 08002 • (609) 667-4644

CHIEF D'AMICO,
YOUR GROUP IS
WELCOMED TO PARTICIPATE.
210 INVITATIONS WERE SENT
TO ALL S.J. MUNICIPALITIES :
TOWNSHIPS AND BOROUGHS.
THIS IS THE FIRST
S.J. REGIONAL
PARADE — A SALUTE TO THE
NATION. IT WILL BE
A GRAND EVENT !!!!
PLEASE JOIN US!
Joe Zanghi

April 3, 1991

Dear Mayor, Council Members,

   We are extending an invitation to your municipality to participate in the 19th annual Cherry Blossom Parade, held in Cherry Hill, N.J. scheduled for May 5th, 1991 with a rain date of May 19th.

   We want this year's parade to be a southern New Jersey regional salute to our Nation and to our honored veterans, past and present. We will dedicate this parade to the American Family" from which we draw our national strength. They are the "Heart" of America.

   We are hoping for 100 percent participation. We will be as one people expressing our national pride and love for this great country.

   We want your town to be represented in this patriotic event. We would like to see your township's flag or banner proudly waving in this parade. We invite all your families that have loved ones in the military and still serving in the Persian Gulf. Any other parade entry, including the Mayor and Council members, will be welcomed!!

   We hope that you will support this endeavor. It will give all townships an opportunity to be a part of this grand salute to our victorious troops and to our great country.

   We will be as one people, drawn together as proud Americans!! On this proud occasion---let us all cross over our township boundaries and join hands. Let's make this year's Cherry Blossom Parade---a grand event for all proud Americans.

   Please join us!! Let your town---"BE AS AMERICAN AS IT CAN BE!!"

                                        Sincerely,

                                        Joseph G. Zanghi
                                        Joseph G. Zanghi
                                        Cherry Blossom Parade

The Largest and Most Spectacular Parade in the State of New Jersey . . . Since 1973

19TH ANNUAL CHERRY BLOSSOM PARADE

Cherry Hill, NJ

As **AMERICAN** as you can get . . .

TROOPS **WELCOME HOME!!**

Block Party!
Military Parade!

Chapel Ave.
May 5th, 1991

All Cherry Hill schools, organizations, businesses, ethnic groups. . .
PROUD AMERICANS, WELCOME!!

A unified community to share the joys of national pride, victory, and worldwide peace.

667-4644

Over the past 19 years **The Cherry Blossom Parade and Festival** was designed to unify the people of Cherry Hill in a proud awareness of our home town!!

This year this traditional event will salute and recognize all of the United States Armed Services . . . *ALL* **our honored veterans, past and present**. . . and the **American families** on which we draw our national strength!!

Let us all come together . . . **PROUDLY!!**

Come join us . . . Be as AMERICAN as you can be!!

Donations Needed!!   Payable to: Cherry Blossom Parade • 16 Pebble Lane • Cherry Hill, NJ 08002

أوقف القتال الان، حافظ على حياتك

عن الملجأ، يجب على حامله التقيد بالخطوات التالية:

للبحث بالسلام

١. اسحب مخزن الذخيرة من سلاحك

سلاحك على كتفك الايسر مع توجيه الماسورة الى الاسفل

٢. احمل

٢. ارفع يديك فوق رأسك

من مواقع القوات المتعددة الجنسيات ببطء وفي قائد

٤. اقترب

المقدمة يرفع هذه الوثيقة فوق رأسه.

٥. اذا عملت هذا تنجو من الموت.

CEASE RESISTANCE - BE SAFE

To seek refuge safely, the bearer must strictly adhere to the following procedures:

1. Remove the magazine from your weapon.

2. Sling your weapon over your left shoulder, muzzle down.

3. Have both arms raised above your head.

4. Approach the Multi - National Forces positions slowly, with the lead soldier holding this document above his head.

5. If you do this, you will not die.

THE MILITARY WIFE
THE LORD'S MOST PERFECT CREATION?

The good Lord was creating a model for military wives and was into his sixth day of overtime when an angel appeared. She said,"Lord, you seem to be having a lot of trouble with this one. What's wrong with the standard model"?

The Lord replied, "Have you seen the specs on this order? She has to be completely independent, possess the qualities of both father and mother, be a perfect hostess to four or 40 with a hour's notice, run on black coffee, handle every emergency imagnable without a manual, be able to carry on cheerfully, even if she is pregnant and has the flu, and she must be willing to move to a new location 10 times in 17 years. And oh, yes she must have six pairs of hands."

The angel shook her head. "six pair of hands? No Way."

The Lord continued, "Don't worry, we will make other military wives to help her. And we will give her an unusually strong heart so it can swell with pride in her husband's achievements, sustain the pain of separations, beat soundly when it is overworked and tired, and be large enough to say 'I understand' when she doesn't, and say 'I love you,' regardless."

"Lord," said the angel, touching his arm gently, "go to bed and get some rest. You can finish this tommorrow."

"I can't stop now." said the Lord. "I am close to creating something unique. Already this model heals herself when she is sick, can put up six unexpected guest for the weekend, wave goodbye to her husband from a pier, a runway or a depot, and understand why it's important that he leave."

The angel circled the model of the military wife, Looked at it closely and sighed, "It looks fine, but it's to soft." "She might look soft." replied the Lord, "but she has the strength of a lion. You would not believe what she can endure."

Finally the angel bent over and ran her finger across the cheek of the Lord's creation. "There's a leak." she announced. Something is wrong with this construction. I am not surprised that it has cracked. You are trying to put to much into this model."

The Lord appeared offended at the angel's lack of confidence. "What you see is not a leak." he said "it's a tear."

"A tear? What is that for?" asked the angel.

The Lord replied,"it's for joy, sadness, pain,disappointment,lonelinuss, pride nd dedication to all the values that she and her husband hold dear."

You are a genius!" exclaimed the angel.

The Lord looked puzzled and replied, "I didn't put it there."

Author Unknown

Military, volunteers quick t[...]

By W.L. HAACKER
PRESS COASTAL MONMOUTH BUREAU

LITTLE DID Thomas Jefferson know when he included in the Declaration of Independence a line pledging "our lives, our fortunes and our sacred honor," how often that promise would be renewed.

Most recently, it was renewed by U.S. servicemen and women in the Persian Gulf War, and what they found was just how much of their family fortunes would be sacrificed in service to their nation.

However, both the federal and state governments are moving quickly to correct the deficiencies.

The problem is that when the U.S. military moved to an all-volunteer force in the 1970s, it was forced to rely heavily on National Guard and reserve units in times of national emergency.

The war against Iraq was the first major test of the military's doctrine of "Total Force Readiness," which requires guard and reserve units to be every bit as good as the regular military.

"We've called up dribs and drabs in the past, but never the thousands we've had to call up this time," said Lt. Col. Elizabeth Yull, statewide family coordinator for the New Jersey National Guard.

Military officials have said some 4,500 New Jerseyans were called to duty in the Persian Gulf.

That large call-up has shown some of the shortcomings of the total force system, although those deficiencies are being addressed for the long term at the federal and state levels, and in the short term by volunteers at individual posts and armories, she said.

Also, most branches of the military have ways of helping their own.

> **‖A lot of families are having financial problems and are getting along OK. Not everyone is a sad story.‖**
>
> **Lt. Col. Elizabeth Yull**
> NEW JERSEY NATIONAL GUARD

Problems faced by reservists and guard members include: a loss of earning power when going from a civilian job to the military; financial pressure because of mortgage debts and rents; child care; and insurance hassles.

At the state level, she said, the Assembly Veterans' Affairs and Military Committee has been holding hearings throughout the state to learn about the problems and how they could be solved.

"Not everyone is having a problem," Lt. Col. Yull cautioned. "The CNN tendency is to seek out the sad story. A lot of families are having financial problems and are getting along OK. Not everyone is a sad story."

However, some 23 guard and reserve families in Monmouth and Ocean counties and some 200 in the state [...] having difficulty making ends me[...] according to volunteer organization[...]

Last month, the Food Bank of M[...] mouth and Ocean Counties loaned [...] not-for-profit status to the Cen[...] Jersey Family Support Group, [...] emergency food pantry set up at [...] National Guard station in Sea Gir[...] aid families of reservists and gu[...] members.

According to Alfred J. Sheppard [...] the food bank's executive directo[...] was something the food bank did w[...] out hesitation.

"This is our country and those[...] need shouldn't feel deserted beca[...] they are called back into service [...] us," he said. "We each have a stak[...] seeing the armed forces are ma[...] tained. We must go the extra mile[...] make sure those who have dedica[...] their lives to us know that their fa[...] lies are being taken care of at home.[...]

Sheppard said he expected finan[...] pressure on military family to conti[...] long after breadwinners had retur[...] from the Persian Gulf.

The food bank, based in Spring L[...] distributes some 50,000 pounds of f[...] a month to 180 agencies in the t[...] county area that feed about 1,[...] families.

"We owe it to them to take car[...] their families while they are gon[...] agreed Gail Goddard, who runs the [...] Girt food pantry. Mrs. Goddard is [...] wife of Master Sgt. James Godda[...] who is stationed at the N.J. Milit[...] Academy, at Sea Girt.

Manasquan reaches out to "Gulf" families

In a ceremony held at the Manasquan Elks Lodge #2534 on April 13, Past Exalted Ruler E. (Woody) Vail and Ron De Luca, newly installed Exalted Ruler, presented a check in the amount of $1,114 to Gale Goddard, Family Coordinator for The Desert Storm/Desert Shield Family Foundation of Sea Girt; Master Sgt. James Goodard and Major Michael Puca, Deputy Commander of the N.J. Military Academy.

The Manasquan Elks, under chairmanship of Vail, raised the money by running a dinner-dance and by selling lapel pins of the U.S. flag and yellow ribbons, in honor of our U.S. Desert Storm troops.

Goodard, in accepting the Elks contribution, stated that the monies would be used to provide financial assistance to New Jersey families of Desert Storm troops who are in need.

She and Major Puca presented a plaque to Vail and De Luca, in appreciation for the Elks effort and support. De Luca, in accepting the award, said, "The B.P.O. Elks have always and will continue to support our troops and the veterans of our armed conflicts."

HELPING[...]
right, pres[...]
ed in the [...]
Puca.

elp Desert Storm families

rs. Goddard said the Sea Girt
ry is one of four — the others
ed in Jersey City, Hammonton and
e May — that serve about 200
ly families. Since the pantries
ned, they have received support
business and individuals, she said.
t recently, the Manasquan El-
ntary School made a donation.

ere are laws on the books to
ect members of the military, the
rd and the reserves, and their
ies, Lt. Col. Yull said.

e Soldiers and Sailors Civil Relief
became a federal law in 1940.
cally, the law protected military
onnel from foreclosure, lowered
imum interest rates on such debts
ortgages, personal loans and
it cards to 6 percent and offered
ts for rent.

ne other law is the Veterans Re-
loyment Act, which holds a job for
ard member or reservist called
to active duty.

he laws need updating and correc-
of new inequities that have come
ght, said Rep. Chris Smith, R-N.J.,
ember of the House Veterans'
rs Committee.

mith said Thursday that a House
— an updated version of the sol-
rs and sailors law — had been
varded to President Bush for his
ected signature.

What came across in testimony,"
th said, "is that we had to get our
together on benefits . . . not six
ths or a year after they returned.
ould have been unconscionable not

CELESTE LA BROSSE/Asbury Park Press

Gail Goddard, volunteer coordinator, stocks shelves of emergency food pantry at the National Guard station, Sea Girt.

EROES—At far left, PER Woody Vail and new ER Ron DeLuca, second from ale Goddard with a donation to help the families of our troops who have serv- ulf. Also with Goodard were Master Sgt. James Goodard and Major Michael

Kudos for 328th from Saudi Arabia

(328th Trans. Det. left to right: Spc Gary Stoeffler, Spc J.C. Dixon, 1st Lt. Michael McLean and Sgt. 1st Class Frank Marchetti)

Photo by John A. Guarascio/444th PAD

MEMORANDUM FOR Adjutant General for the State of New Jersey

SUBJECT: RESERVE COMPONENTS CALLED TO ACTIVE DUTY

1. As the Commander of the 330th Movement Control Center (MCC), 1st COSCOM, XVIII Airborne Corps, now in Saudi Arabia, I pass along my compliments on providing an outstanding team of soldiers who make up the 328th Transportation Movement Control Detachment (Mount Holly). They have been assigned to my command since their arrival in support of Operation Desert Shield.

2. MCC's are traditionally very dependent upon the Reserve Components. Mine is no exception. I cannot accomplish my mission without them. The 328th, commanded by Second Lieutenant Michael McLean, has been made an integral part of the MCC. The concept of operation involves locating his detachment, or Movement Control Team (MCT), along with one of the forward Corps Support Groups (CSG) of the COSCOM. The MCT and CSG form a habitual relationship in providing logistic support of one of the Combat Divisions (and non-Divisional units on an area basis). The MCT provides movement management of the numerous transportation assets assigned to the CSG. Although these are primarily wheeled vehicles, they are also responsible for managing the movement of Army cargo and passengers by both Army and Air Force aircraft.

3. To date, Michael McLean and his soldiers have done a magnificent job and are to be commended. We on the Active component side know these patriots have sacrificed much by leaving their jobs and families. They are truly great examples of the Total Army Concept we have heard so much of. It is working! You and the people of the State of New Jersey can be justifiably proud of the well trained soldiers of the 328th. The flag of the State of New Jersey these soldiers brought with them flies proudly.

4. Feel free to share my thanks with the families and friends of these great soldiers.

DAVID W. NEDELA
LTC(P), TC
Commanding

This tree is in honor of
our men and women on
active duty in the
Persian Gulf.
GODSPEED

SPC DOUGLAS M. CABLER
PV2 GREGORY A. DICK
PFC FRANK GOODWIN
SSG FRANK HOLLAND   1T ANTHONY PEACOCK
SSG JOHN A. KILL   2LT WILLIAM L. DEMAR
SPC SCOTT LUBER   SGT ROSEANNE POLNIK
SN DAVID McGOUGH   SPC RORY RADELA
SPC LAURENCE MURDOCK   SGT JOSEPH TEREZNO
SPC FREDERICK MERKEL   SEC MIKE VEY
MS2 JACK MAURER   SP4 DAVID WILLIAMS

PROUD MOMENT: Last week's lighting of the tree at the Crest Pier was dedicated to those men and women of the community serving with the National Guard's 253rd Transportation Unit. Billy Peace proudly points out his dad's name on the list next to the tree.

Photo by Jean Barraclough

HANDIWORK: The Sunday evening youth group, made up of young to mid-teens, created this 'show of hands' show of support on the front lawn of the United Methodist Church in Cape May Court House.

Banner Day

A BANNER DAY - Families of the 144th Supply Company and residents of New Jersey came out to support the unit's deployment along the many roads to Fort Dix.

Desert Shield: N.J. Answers the Call

By John A. Guarascio/444th PAD

On August 7, 1990, at approximately 0130 hours, the Department of Defense asked for, and Governor Jim Florio approved, the use of aircraft and airmen from the 170th Air Refueling Group for participation in the defense of Saudi Arabia. By 0200 hours the "call" went out for volunteers and by 0400 hours aircrafts and crews were on the flight line awaiting further orders. Within a span of two hours the alert and response capability of the New Jersey Air National Guard was challenged and showed itself more than equal to the task.

The operation called "Desert Shield" proved to be the largest mobilization action of United States military forces since the Vietnam War. According to Major General Vito Morgano, the Adjutant General, "Our New Jersey Guardmembers were among the first asked to participate in support of 'Desert Shield.' They responded with the speed, professionalism and spirit that has become a standard by which all subsequently called units could be measured."

The aircraft flown by the 170th AREFG is the KC-135E Stratotanker. This plane has been described as the "big gas station in the sky." It has the capability of refueling United States Air Force aircraft while in flight. The 170th AREFG trains routinely for world-wide missions and comes under the authority of the Strategic Air Command while serving on Active Duty.

Since the mission, number of aircraft, number of guardmembers, location and mission duration were classified, the rumors and speculation began taking its toll on not only New Jersey's soldiers and airmen but on their families.

"In order to ease the uncertainties and fears of families, I called upon every asset available to answer questions for our guardmembers. We used our Employer Support of the Guard and Reserve Committee to respond to employment concerns, our Family Assistance Coordinator to answer health insurance and family questions and our Judge Advocate fielded all legal questions. Numerous press briefings and television interviews were given to insure the facts were properly presented," Morgano said.

Although much information was disseminated and constant efforts were made to counter erroneous reports, "Murphy's Law" did surface on occasion. One newspaper ran an article listing all the New Jersey National Guard units "available to deploy" - but the typesetter left out the word "available." An elected official released a list of units he "felt" could be called to active duty. This caused reporters from both the print and television media to rush in droves to those units and disrupt training.

With all the fanfare our guardmembers were sought out for interviews and photographs. Governor Jim Florio, visiting the 170th AREFG to thank his troops for their efforts and dedication, was "greeted" by 45 reporters and was caught up in an "information frenzy." But through it all our "citizen-soldiers" performed their missions and took the confusion in stride.

"The resourcefulness and ability to work under the constant pressure that our guardmembers displayed is an unending source of pride for me. They managed to work through all the disruptions and never lost sight of their mission or of its importance," said Morgano.

As this is going to press, we do not know what, if any, other New Jersey units will be called into active service, but if "Past is Prologue" this nation knows New Jersey will provide units that are second to none.

ANSWERING THE CALL - A KC-135E Stratotanker from the 170th AREFG is shown performing the same type of missions required during the units role in operation "Desert Shield." photo by 170th AREFG

M1A1's get "Desert Storm" touch

By David Moore 444th PAD

*W*hen it came time to prepare, repaint, and pack 60 tanks for Operation Desert Shield, Army personnel at the Tank Automotive Command, Michigan (TACOM), had their eyes on the Garden State's Army and Air National Guard members to get the job done.

When the command's eyes blinked all the M1A1 Abrams were prepared for duty in the Middle East several days in advance of the deadline.

In addition, the Department of Defense saved more than $100,000, according to estimates.

But it was no small feat repainting the woodland green tanks with Chemical Agent Resistant Covering in the sand color. Before any tank preparation could be done, a location had to be found. The tanks at the Military Ocean Terminal in Bayonne had arrived from Europe. The terminal was one location and McGuire AFB was another site under consideration to get the tanks ready for desert duty.

The terminal was chosen and a vacant warehouse was prepared by terminal personnel so the tanks could be painted. Some of the work included repair to doors, the installation of overhead electrical lights and cleaning the floor so there was room for the work.

For what many officials believe is the first time in New Jersey National Guard history, both Army and Air Guard members joined together at the terminal to accomplish the mission.

Photo by 108th TFW PAO
A LITTLE AROUND THE EDGES - Staff Sgt. Ronald T. Riddick of Co. D. 250th SBM, tapes one of the 60 M1A Abrahms tanks to be painted for Desert Storm. Members of the Army and Air National Guard participated in the joint mission.

The goal was to repaint 10 tanks a day. During the first two days however, the assembly line process was slow. But after the "bugs" were worked out and procedures established, everyone operated at full speed.

Col. Jon F. Gribbin, surface maintenance manager, said key factors in overcoming the problems were quickly overcome by the willingness and dedication of the personnel involved in the painting mission. In all, 28 members of the Army National Guard and 11 Air National Guard members of the 108th Tactical Fighter Wing and 170th Refueling Group tackled the job. The Army National Guard members who participated were from the 250th SBM, 250th Sig. Bn., 50th Spt. Bn., 117th HEM Co., Det. 1 150th FSB.

"What we did was utilize the Army National Guard members to prepare the tanks for painting, while the Air Guard using their specialized spray equipment from McGuire AFB painted the tanks," Gribbin said.

"Everyone worked very hard and worked long hours to complete the mission," he added.

All painting and preparation for shipment was completed by Oct. 9.

"Everything went extremely well. We finished several days before the goal date," Gribbin said.

Gribbin said one unique element of the job was that as a result of the joint effort between the Army and Air National Guard, the Air Guard members would be receiving the Army Achievement Medal, while foremen on the job would receive the Army Commendation Medal.

Based on Gribbin's after action report, his recommendations are that future projects should be reviewed to ascertain if the project could be worked in a joint venture to promote better understanding and a feeling of togetherness between the two commands.

"The outstanding results achieved in the joint accomplishment of this mission proves that it can be done with professional results," Gribbin's report concludes.

When breadwinners go off to fight

Congress is mulling over a stack of bills to ease the financial burden on military families

Many reservists accustomed to civilian salaries are sending home considerably leaner military pay from the Middle East these days. Pile on new costs, like suddenly heavier child-care expenses, and many military families can no longer keep the household balance sheet in balance. Chief Warrant Officer Harry Lee of Ventura, Calif., for example, earned $3,800 a month as a federal public-affairs officer before he answered the call. Now he earns $3,400, and his wife, Dorothy, is working longer hours at a second job. Even career soldiers, whose basic pay remains steady in war and peace, are being hit by added expenses, including phone bills that often top $500 a month.

The pinch has been duly noted in Washington. Enlisted men and women needn't pay federal income tax on wages earned since January 17, the day after the war started; officers are exempt for the first $500 of each month's salary. And all service people in the gulf can divert up to $10,000 from their pay to special military savings plans that pay 10 percent interest, about four points higher than most money-market accounts. That is just the beginning of a wave of relief legislation. More than 50 bills are pending in Congress that could shift even more money and benefits directly to soldiers and their families. Some could be passed as early as March, others will trickle along. Congress watchers say the following proposals are the most likely to succeed.

Compensation
■ Soldiers in combat zones would receive an increase in "imminent danger" pay from $110 to $150 a month. Saudi Arabia is a combat zone; Germany, where many troops are serving, is not.
■ The payment if a military person dies in the gulf would double to $6,000.
■ Life-insurance benefits would double to $100,000.

Medical and child-care benefits
■ The federal government would pay all or part of the expense of private insur-ance for families who choose not to join the military health plan.
■ A proposal now on the table to triple military health-insurance deductibles, currently at $50 per person and $100 per family each year, would be postponed until the war ends.

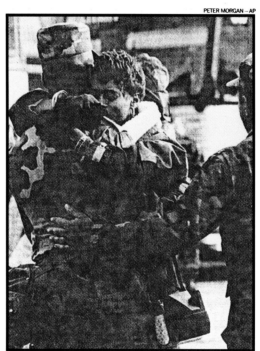

PETER MORGAN – AP

Long goodbye. *Besides the personal anguish, many military families must face financial problems.*

■ The government would pay a portion of child-care costs.

Prewar debts
The Soldiers and Sailors Civil Relief Act of 1940 already affords some protection against financial obligations left behind by those sent to the Persian Gulf. For example, military personnel who can prove financial hardship related to the war may be eligible for a reduced interest rate of 6 percent annually on all pre-combat outstanding loans, including credit-card balances and mortgages. The law also allows them to postpone scheduled court proceedings, terminate leases early, postpone monthly payments on installment loans under certain circumstances and be protected against foreclosure if they fail to make mortgage payments. Detailed information on the law is available from state and local bar associations, who also can provide free or low-cost legal help to military families who are battling creditors. New provisions might include:
■ Families whose monthly rent is $1,200 or less would be protected against eviction or harassment. The current cap, established after World War II, is $150 a month. The government will not pay the rent for families in arrears, but it will see to it that they are not evicted.
■ Soldiers paying off student loans could suspend payments until after the war; reservists who left classes in midsemester would be refunded their tuition.

Some states have been more zealous than the federal government in coming to reservists' defense. Pennsylvania, for example, recently passed a law requiring employers to cover all health-insurance costs for reservists and National Guard members for 30 days after they are called to duty. This eliminates gaps in medical coverage while reservists are waiting for military health plans to kick in. The governor's office in each state can tell questioners where to get information on state-specific laws.

Because the military typically alerts soldiers to new laws and provisions through announcements in their pay envelopes, many families may have trouble keeping abreast of changes. Several service organizations issue bulletins and newsletters that track new laws. Membership costs about $20 annually per group. They include: Reserve Officers Association, One Constitution Avenue, N.E., Washington, DC 20002, (202) 479-2200; Non-Commissioned Officers Association, 225 N. Washington Street, Alexandria, VA 22314, (703) 549-0311, and the National Military Family Association, 6000 Stevenson Avenue, Suite 304, Alexandria, VA 22304-3526, (703) 823-6632.

Sometimes help comes without waiting and red tape. When Dorothy Lee's bankers heard her husband had been sent to the Persian Gulf, they wrapped her car loan in a yellow ribbon – and eliminated her interest payments. ■

BY FRANCESCA LUNZER KRITZ

Arabian Knights: 328th and 253rd mobilize

By David Moore/444th PAD

Approximately 140 members of two N.J. National Guard Units, arrived with dufflebags in hand, at Ft. Dix on September 30th for final processing. These were their last steps before their final destination — Saudi Arabia. Their mission is to support military forces as part of Operation Desert Shield.

The units reporting for duty were the 136 member 253rd Transportation Company in Cape May Court House and the four-member 328th Transportation Detachment in Pemberton Township.

During a briefing on Thursday, September 27th, at the Cape May Court House Armory, the words "M-Day" were written on the blackboard followed by "needed equipment preparation." "I never thought I would see that, but now that it is here, we have a job to do," said Maj. Michael Puca, Troop Command's support supervisor, as he addressed the unit's officers and senior noncommissioned officers.

Both units had been put on alert September 23rd, and received their mobilization orders to Ft. Dix. The 253rd is a light and medium transportation unit, while the Pemberton detachment plans transportation and supply routes for military vehicles. "It's been very busy around here for quite sometime," Puca emphasized.

"...now that it is here, we have a job to do."

Security around the armory has been tight with armed Cape May police.

"Our detachment found final preparation very easy. We are a small outfit so everything is in order. Other than the anxiety of separating from our friends and family we are ready to serve," said 1st LT. John McLean, Commander of the 328th.

Col. Dom Trocchia, Troop Command's commander, told members of the 253rd "The entire National Guard stands behind

THE REAL DEAL — Ralph Lonergan of the 253rd Transportation Company, Cape May Court House, briefs his unit for mobilization to Fort Dix where last minute processing was being completed before the final destination—Saudi Arabia.

you and your families. The country and New Jersey are also behind you."

While unit members were being briefed, many of them were outside in the hallway waiting to take care of personal affairs.

A bank representative from Cape May Savings was on hand to take care of unit members' financial affairs by providing direct deposit service.

"The entire community is supporting the unit," Puca said.

Sgt. Roseann Pollini, 20, the 253rd's clerk, was preparing her legal package which included power of attorney and her first will.

She said her family in Wildwood Crest, where she lives with six of her ten brothers and sisters, have difficulty coming to terms with the possibility of war.

"At first I was scared, but now I'm willing to go," she said. "We're always training, We're ready."

Maj. Joseph M. Scaturo, a Monmouth

County attorney said, "I have not seen a unit with higher morale. These folks are capable of carrying out any task they are assigned."

"Naturally, they do not want to go to war, but they're proud to take part in Operation Desert Shield." Trocchia said after the briefing.

Puca explained that during the mobilization process, Guard member's families were given briefings to try to take the pressure off the period of separation and a 24 hour hotline had been established.

He also said that while Guard members are on active duty, the local Coast Guard in Cape May has volunteered to provide medical care to the local National Guard families.

This was the second time in a month that members had been away from their families. A month prior, about 4,000 of the New Jersey National Guard's Troop Command, including both of the activated units, completed their annual two-week training in Camp Shelby, Mississippi

Secretary of Defense Armed Forces Day Message

by Dick Cheney
Secretary of Defense

O'er the land of the free and the home of the brave.

*A*s Secretary of Defense, I'm proud to extend a well deserved tribute to all of you who have been willing to put on our nation's uniform and go in harm's way for your fellow citizens. This day is set aside each year to recognize the dedication, professionalism, and the sacrifices of our military. During the Persian Gulf war, those qualities were displayed in a hundred different ways for all Americans to see.

Each of you can be proud of your accomplishments. You are part of a victorious armed force that saved freedom for the Kuwaiti people. Your courage and devotion to duty are second to none.

When I visit you stationed throughout our country and around the world, I am constantly struck by your professionalism and enthusiasm. The all-volunteer force is a success and the whole world now has enormous respect for your ability to get the job done. These past months have been difficult and have called upon your reserves of courage and determination. Your accomplishment in this struggle has brought renewed pride for our military and for our nation. Your standards of excellence and superior performance have become a model for all Americans. ✈

CINCSAC Message: "To the Men & Women of the 170th Air Refueling Group"

*D*esert Shield and Desert Storm have tested the mettle of everyone in America. In particular those of us who have been deeply, directly and emotionally involved have felt the impact more than most.

I define the role of SAC as a "Twin Peaks" phenomenon. One peak is that of nuclear deterrence, which by the way, we have climbed, won and continue to win, while the other peak is one of global force-projection allowing us to come to the defense of those whom our national leadership have selected for our favor. Only by keeping both "peaks" sharp can we continue to provide the defense America has a right to expect.

Your role was key to keeping the nuclear deterrent peak pointed in the proper direction. Your sacrifice was necessary in order for the other segment of our force-projection assets to carry out their assigned role without worrying about leaving the free world at risk from a nuclear surprise. Your quiet professionalism shouted out your dedication to mission, country, and command. I take this opportunity to formally say "Thank You" for sharing your capabilities with those of us on permanent active duty.

I appreciate the opportunity to be your CINCSAC in large measure because it gives me the chance to rub shoulders, exchange ideas, and work with quality people such as you and yours. Your sacrifice from careers, home life and standard comforts did not go unnoticed. I and the American people saw them and we appreciate your efforts.

George L. Butler, General
Commander in Chief

Desert Dispatches

Major Terrance C. Holliday
170 AREFG

With a sudden, yet relieving thud, the inbound KC-135E Stratotanker from the 170th Air Refueling Group had arrived in eastern Saudi Arabia to participate in Operation Desert Shield. Although the 170th has been an active player in this historic military event since August 1990, it marked the first time that any of us on that aircraft had become directly involved. As we flew over the deserts of the Middle East and discussed the contrasts of the topography, we also shared our concerns and expectations of this very different type of Temporary Duty.

Chief Master Sergeant Craig Czarnecki and Master Sergeant James Gallagher, both of the 170th Consolidated Aircraft Maintenance Squadron, expressed a willingness to make a small, yet positive impact on the Air National Guard mission. Everyone was well aware of the importance of the mission to which we were assigned. As the cargo hatch opened and we were greeted by the aerial port personnel and persuaded to form a baggage chain, the cool dryness of the cabin was quickly replaced with heat and humidity. My first glimpse through those doors, revealed an impressive number of Air National Guard KC-135E aircraft. Each was bedecked with respective state tail and boom identifications. Many were adorned with nose art. Our bird was the *Ace's High*.

Once we loaded and unloaded our bags a few more times, we finally settled in. It was a shower, to bed and then to work. We were assigned to the 1701st Air Refueling Wing, Provisional. It has since been redesignated the 1701st Strategic Wing. The wing is unique in that its personnel is comprised of active duty, Air National Guard and Air Force Reserve members. The commander is Colonel Charles M. Baier of the 190th AREFG, Kansas Air National Guard. Many of the key positions have been filled on a temporary duty rotational basis. With unit activations, this personnel structure is likely to change.

Since Operation Desert Shield is an ongoing exercise, there remains a great deal that we cannot discuss. What can be said is that the Air National Guard and specifically, the 170th Air Refueling Group is performing its mission admirably. Unlike prior deployments, there is a great deal more work and precious little time for relaxation. For many of us, this is a first or at least, infrequent, Christmas away from our families. Although I said so long to the *Ace's High* as Majors Paul Alvater, Chip Morgan and Dennis O'Connell flew westward, I was saying hello to Captain Dana Darby and the crew on *Jersey Girl*. And so it continued.

The cooperation that we have all enjoyed under these difficult circumstances has been extraordinary. The "can do attitude" and positive interaction on all levels has been the difference in the overwhelming success that this challenging mission has enjoyed. I have never witnessed such a demonstration that reinforces the concept of "Total Force" as I have seen here in Saudi Arabia. Our Saudi friends and allies have taught us to say "Bukara, inshaalah", which means "Tomorrow, God willing".

> **❝**
>
> *I have never witnessed such a demonstration that reinforces the concept of Total Force...*
>
> **❞**

Color Guard - 253rd Transportation Company

Invocation - Major Daniel Ricketts

253rd Transportation Company

Master of Ceremonies- George Magnavita

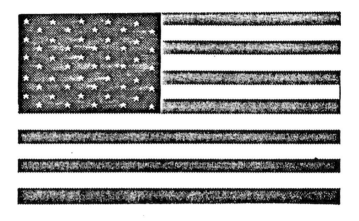

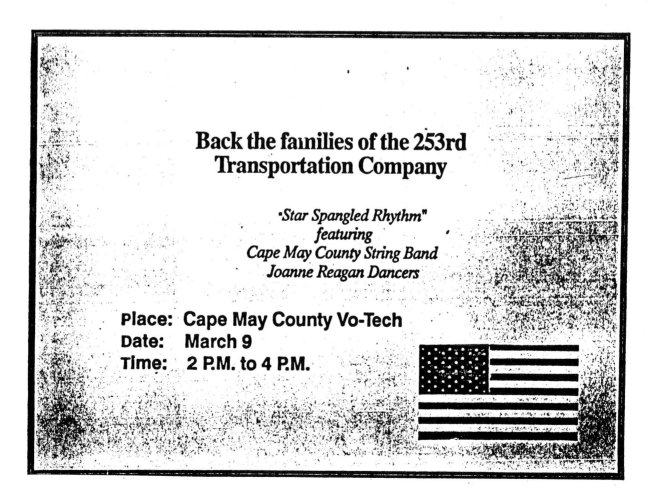

Back the families of the 253rd Transportation Company

"Star Spangled Rhythm"
featuring
Cape May County String Band
Joanne Reagan Dancers

Place: Cape May County Vo-Tech
Date: March 9
Time: 2 P.M. to 4 P.M.

BEEF BEER

BENEFITS

253RD Transportation Co.

DATE: SATURDAY, FEB. 16, 1991

SUNDANCE NIGHT CLUB

3400 NEW JERSEY AVE. WILDWOOD

DOOR PRIZES

Family

RAFFLES

ENTERTAINMENT *Support* MUSIC

Group

DONATIONAL SALES

7PM-1AM   DONATION AT DOOR- $10.00

For Which It Stands

**To The Men And Women Of The
144th Supply Company, N.J.A.N.G.
And To All Who Served The U.S.A.
During The 1991 Persian Gulf War**

**Erected By
Hammonton Lions Club
May 18, 1991
"We Serve"**

Expressions Of Hope

On The Homefront

OPERATION DESERT STORM

STARS AND STRIPES RALLY

FEBRUARY 16, 1991

"CAPE MAY COUNTY
SUPPORTS OUR TROOPS"

PRAYER
FOR SERVICE MEN AND WOMEN

*Oh Almighty God, whose great power
and eternal wisdom embraces the universe,
watch over all servicemen and women.
Protect them from harm in the performance
of their duty. We recommend them to your
loving care because their duty is dangerous.
Grant them your unending strength and
courage in their daily assignments.
Dear God, protect these brave
men and women.
Grant them your almighty protection
and unite them safely with their families
after their duty has ended.
Amen.*

Composed by Marie Kill
Her son, Sgt. John Kill, is serving with the
National Guard 253rd Transport

Super Bowl
Sunday

Meadowlands

"Wings"

I have climbed the heights of nature.
Conquered valleys cold and steep:
And often felt there's nothing to
look forward to but sleep.

I have battled mind and body
just to find a strength renewed:
I have weathered endless chow lines,
and I've tasted better food.

My bones are one big toothache,
and in pain my eyes are racked!
And with luck under the callouses,
my feet are still in tact.

I have learned to swallow pride
that even boxers couldn't match.

"Oh!" "What Price Airborne, schooled by
men with faces that could kill!
Demanding even unknown strength,
and purchasing my will.

The next thing I recall, I was
Among the chosen few,
that said good-bye to earthly green,
then darted for the blue.

My mind takes inventory of the
things that I've been taught.
Uncommon faces by my side,
Yet, sharing common thought.

Then suddenly a strong command
and jumpers pierce the sky.
And that's the time you pray the most,
and wish that you could fly.

As anxious chills make their debut,
thus, taxing my control,
My heart begins to sense, "It's time,"
And plays a drummers roll.

The dreaded moment has arrived;
No prayers will help me now.
As concentration forces icy sweat
across my brow.

"Go!" How well delivered was that,
"No turn back" command.
As my body like a piston plunges
straight for "no man's land."

Just timing, nothing more is what,
enshrouds my "perfect" mind.
T'ween God and sand I plummet;
Leaving safety far behind.

As precious seconds take their leave,
my mind is now a sword;
A sharpened master of my fate,
commanding, "Pull the cord!"

With strength that equalled Grecian lore,
I pulled for all my worth.
And prayed like I have never prayed,
as closer came the earth.

And then the sudden "JERK!"
My body jumps with awesome power.
Left little doubt that God,
would see me through my finest hour.

To everything there is a season,
and in time I'll reminisce.
Of weighted packs while climbing high,
and crawling through abyss.

I'll think of iron discipline,
I'd never known before.
And chow lines standing in the cold;
all tired, tired, and sore.

I'll think of squirming in the mud.
in overbearing stench.
And that demon's thirst for water,
mere canteens could never quench.

But most of all, I'll think about,
the jump I took that day;
The loving push God gave me,
and his presence all the way.

Now some will ask if I would,
do it over if I could.
And I'd reply, "You see these wings?"   **Written By Michael Carl**
"YOU DAMN RIGHT BET I WOULD!" **Leyva In Honor Of**
Jacque Green.

Signs
Of
Support

On The Homefront

Patriot Rally
in Support of the Troops

February 23, 1991
Memorial Park in Ocean City

A G.I. Family's Prayer

Hear, Lord, my prayer for G.I.
so eager to live-too young to die.

Beneath an alien blistering sun.
He faces a dangerous enemy gun.

The storm clouds gather, the horror of war, my soldier stands
bravely guarding the door.

Defending justice, peace, and freedom,
to his Commander-in-Chief give Holy wisdom.

From wars' alarms, bring swift release.
Hasten the day of honorable peace.

On land and sand and sea and air.
I back my soldier with this prayer.

"No matter how far he's forced to roam,
just bring, I pray, my G.I. home."

Amen

Robert H. Schuller
January 1991

This Is A Poem Written By A Marine Named Raymond Santiago Jr. To His Girlfriend, Linda Gonzalez.

"Love"

As you recite these words,
from my heart.
Remember my love,
as we are apart.

For my love is true,
only to you.
It's not because of
your beauty, but the
things you do.

Like your devotion to me,
and tender loving care.
The bondage of true love,
is what we share.

So, pray to the Lord,
that I'll never be harmed.
Because I won't feel safe,
until I'm home in your arms!

Glenwood Avenue School presents check to the 253rd Family Support Group.

4th Grade Class at Enfield Elementary School.

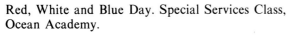

Red, White and Blue Day. Special Services Class, Ocean Academy.

SFC Ed Panny speaks to Enfield Elementary Class on the Gulf crisis.

Hearing Impaired Class at Ocean Academy School made personal yellow ribbons.

Sgt. Joseph Tedesco with pen pals from North School, Brigantine.

CW4 Dan D'Amico presents Mrs. Ann Black a Desert Storm pin.

Student at Ocean Academy School tries on Desert Storm uniform.

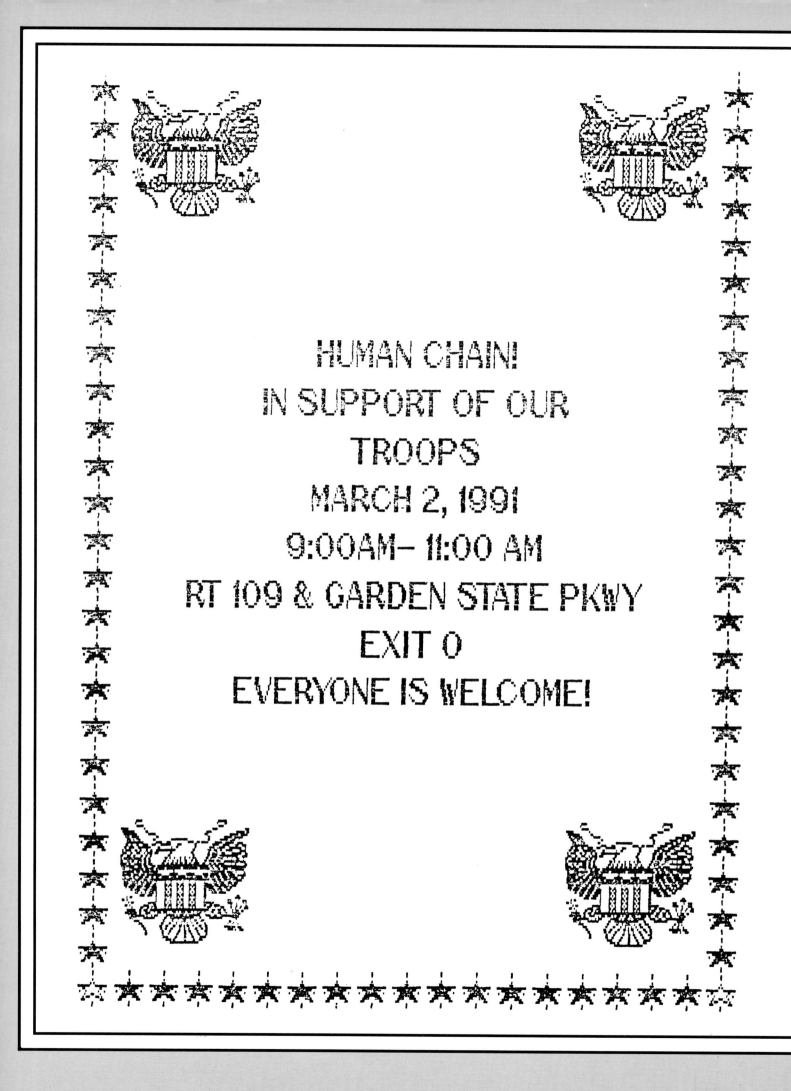

HUMAN CHAIN!
IN SUPPORT OF OUR
TROOPS
MARCH 2, 1991
9:00AM– 11:00 AM
RT 109 & GARDEN STATE PKWY
EXIT 0
EVERYONE IS WELCOME!

THE JERSEY SKEETERS

A Chapter of the Good Sam Club
14 LINDEN ROAD, BURLINGTON, NEW JERSEY 08016.

Sponsors

DESERT SHIELD DROP

Adopt-A-Troop Program

ITEMS REQUESTED ARE:

Playing Cards	Visine	Tissues	Magazines
Scrabble	Eye Wash	Shampoo – Conditioner	Pens – Pencils
Uno	Sun Glasses	Feminine Hygiene	Disposable Razors
Checkers	Sun Visors	Female Undies	Roll-on Deodorants
Chess	Dry Cell Batteries	Female Socks & Slippers	T-Shirts (all sizes)
Monopoly	Liquid Soap	Ladies Razors	Electronic Handheld Games
Yahtzee	Shaving Cream	Talcum Powder	KoolAid Mixes
Squirt Guns	After Shave	Foot Powder	Spring Water
Balls	Tooth Brushes	Combs – Brushes	Ice Tea Mix
Dominoes	Tooth Paste	Q-Tips – Emery Boards	Tang (all flavors)
Darts	Dental Floss	Paper Back Books	Dry Soup Mixes
Cribbage	Mouth Wash	Cassette Tapes (Blank)	Drawing Pencils
Sand Flea Cream	Vaseline	Cassette Music (All Types)	Pads & Paper
Sun Screen Lotion	Antiseptic Cream Stick	Word Search Books	Mens Socks
Lip Balm	Cotton Balls	Crossword Puzzles	Mens Underwear
* DOG FLEA COLLARS			

* NEW REQUEST

DO NOT SEND!
Alcohol – Pork Products – Pornography
Religious Items – Bar Soap – Stick Deodorants
Aerosol Products – Weapons – Glass

FOR MORE INFORMATION CALL:
Sharon Devereaux, 609-723-7162

Thanking
Our
Volunteers

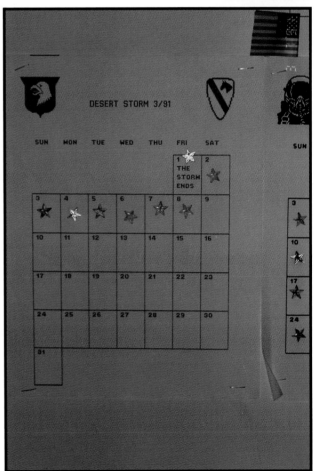

New Jersey Society of Certified Public Accountants

★OPERATION TAX STORM★

The New Jersey Society of Certified Public Accountants (NJSCPA) is serving the members of Operation Desert Storm by offering free tax preparation assistance to the troops and their spouses or designees. **Operation Tax Storm** will aid you in the completion of standard New Jersey and federal tax returns, that may include: wages, salaries, interest and dividend income, and standard or itemized deductions.

Operation Tax Storm is here to help! We understand many families of our troops have been affected financially by one or both spouses being activated. By sharing our accounting expertise, we can help alleviate some of your troubles. The IRS has granted service members a 180 day tax deferral, but that does not help those who are relying on refunds to ease the financial burdens caused by mobilization. This program will continue until all our service members are home.

The Society is working with the command information officer at the department of Military and Veterans' Affairs. This program will encompass <u>all</u> chains of command in New Jersey: the Army, Navy, Air Force, National Guard, Air National Guard, Marine and Coast Guard. To be eligible for free CPA tax preparation assistance in completing 1990 individual or joint state and federal tax returns, the service member must:

1. be a New Jersey resident called to active duty as a result of Operation Desert Storm;
2. not have been released from active duty prior to March 1, 1991;
3. submit a copy of orders calling him/her to active duty.

CPAs from across the state have volunteered for **Operation Tax Storm** in order to meet requests for assistance. All requests will be matched through the NJSCPA headquarters in Roseland. To sign up for the program, all you have to do is fill out the enclosed application with a copy of active duty orders and send it to: NJSCPA, **Operation Tax Storm**, 425 Eagle Rock Avenue, Roseland, NJ 07068. If you simply have a question about your income tax, call Jean O'Connor at the Society, 201/226-4494, and she can refer you to a CPA who will answer your question over the phone.

SERVING THOSE WHO SERVE
OUR COUNTRY

STATE OF NEW JERSEY
DEPARTMENT OF MILITARY AND VETERANS' AFFAIRS
EGGERT CROSSING ROAD, CN 340
TRENTON, NEW JERSEY 08625-0340

28 September 1990

DEPARTMENTAL BULLETIN NO. 16 (Effective until 28 September 1992 unless sooner rescinded or superseded)

DIFFERENTIAL SALARY FOR MOBILIZED NEW JERSEY STATE EMPLOYEES (AD)

1. On 13 September 1990, Governor Jim Florio issued the enclosed Executive Order No. 15.

2. This Executive Order, the first of its kind in the United States, authorizes each member of the New Jersey National Guard or the Reserve Components of the Armed Forces of the United States who is a New Jersey State employee, and who is mobilized in support of Operation Desert Shield, to receive a salary equal to the differential between their State salary and their Military Pay for a period of 180 days. In addition, the mobilized State employees will receive their normal health, life insurance and pension coverage.

3. The provisions of this Executive Order should be brought to the attention of all members of the New Jersey National Guard who are employees of the State of New Jersey as well as all Departmental employees who are members of a Reserve Component.

4. Questions regarding the above should be directed to LTC William C. Lowe, (609) 530-6899.

OFFICIAL:

NICHOLAS C. KING
Major, NJANG (Ret)
Chief, Administrative Services

DISTRIBUTION:
A, A1, A2, A3, B, C, D, E, G2, H

1 Encl

VITO MORGANO
Major General, NJARNG
The Adjutant General

Desert Storm Benefit

Lake Lenape Benefit for Desert Storm families. Cindy Ellis receives check from Miss Mays Landing.

Families enjoy the activities at Lake Lenape.

Saddam in the dunk tank.

Lake Lenape
July 4, 1991

Lake Lenape, Mays Landing.

Trophy winners at Lake Lenape Volleyball Tournament.

Cindy Ellis accepts check at July 4th Lake Lenape fundraiser.

Showing Their Support

On The Homefront

Seven Seals Award Of The ESGR

Butler H.S., Butler, N.J.
Presented By Colonel Evers And SPC Anthony Caffrey

Operation Desert Shield

FREE PORTRAITS

DATE: 6 MARCH 1991

TIME: 6:30 P.M.

WHERE: NATIONAL GUARD ARMORY
(CLASS ROOM)

WHO: SPOUSES, CHILDREN, PARENTS

PROFESSIONAL SERVICE BY

Perfect Exposure from
Ocean City
_____
P.S. Let's surprise HIM/HER with a nice
Portrait

May 21, 1991

Dear Mrs Goddart:

Thank you very much for the help that you have given me and for continuing to help, while I am trying to regain n independency + handle my own affairs.

To this day, I have registered with a few agencies in the area. So far, the temporar assignments I have taken, were only for a few days. I have been told by reps from these agencies that the demand for employment is increasing.

I'm not sure about the amount of assistanc I qualify for, or the number of months I can apply for grants, but any help at all is greatly appreciated.

Sincerely,
M. R. Jones-Puryear.

Family Day Picnic

Interfaith Service

Desert Storm   Desert Shield   Desert Storm   Desert Shield   Desert Storm   Deser

Desert Storm Desert Shield Desert Storm Desert Shield Desert Storm Desert

Shield   Desert   Storm   Desert Shield   Desert Storm   Desert Shield   Desert Storm

Desert Shield Desert Storm Desert Shield Desert Storm Desert Shield Desert

262

OPERATION DESERT STORM

Persian Gulf 1991

Storm   Desert Shield   Desert Storm   Desert Shield   Desert Storm   Desert Shield

WELCOME

263

144th Supply Company Replacements

Last minute details are taken care of by 144th replacements.

The new 144th's 2LT Judie Marranco heads towards plane.

Part of replacements from out of state load gear for transport to airport.

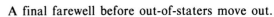

A final farewell before out-of-staters move out.

Out-of-state replacements being deployed with the 144th Supply Company load up gear.

Cpt. Joseph Sarama of the 144th replacements.

Out-of-state replacements ready to join the 144th deployment.

LT Karen Sprague, LT. Leon Yearty, SPC Eugenio Santiago, and CW2 Harry Fullahee being processed with the new 144th.

Replacements during out-processing.

A fare thee well!

Hurry up and wait!

Family farewells.

144th Replacements

Waiting for deployment.

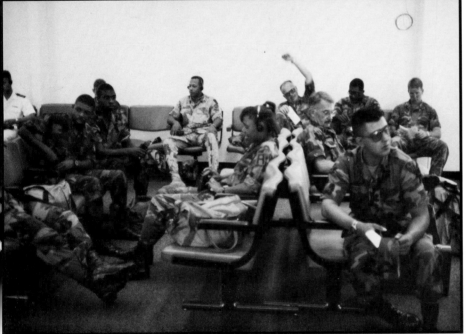

Out-processing.

Out-of-staters loading up.

The 144th Homecoming
At Ft. Dix

144th Homecoming

New Jersey National Guard
Family Assistance Program

Certificate of Appreciation

awarded to

FAMILY SUPPORT VOLUNTEERS

DESERT SHIELD/STORM

This Certificate is presented in recognition of the sacrifices you have made to support the Families of the New Jersey National Guard

Elizabeth Myall

Family Assistance Coordinator

15 January 1991

Date

Vito Morgano

Vito Morgano
Major General, NJARNG
The Adjutant General

272